3800 15 00288060 0

High Life Highland

D0513551

EXTREME ANIMALS

Dominic Couzens

First published in 2015 by Reed New Holland Publishers Pty Ltd
London • Sydney • Auckland

The Chandlery, Unit 9, 50 Westminster Bridge Road, London SE1 7QY, United Kingdom
1/66 Gibbes Street, Chatswood, NSW 2067, Australia
5/39 Woodside Avenue, Northcote, Auckland 0627, New Zealand

www.newhollandpublishers.com

Copyright © 2015 Reed New Holland Publishers Pty Ltd
Copyright © 2015 in text: Dominic Couzens
Copyright © 2015 in photographs: individual photographers as credited on page 181

All rights reserved. No part of this publication may be reproduced, stored in a retrieval system
or transmitted, in any form or by any means, electronic, mechanical, photocopying, recording
or otherwise, without the prior written permission of the publishers and copyright holders.

A record of this book is held at the British Library and the National Library of Australia.

ISBN 978 1 92151 734 1

Managing Director: Fiona Schultz
Publisher and Project Editor: Simon Papps
Designer: Thomas Casey
Production Director: Olga Dementiev
Printer: Toppan Leefung Printing Ltd

10 9 8 7 6 5 4 3 2 1

Keep up with New Holland Publishers on Facebook
www.facebook.com/NewHollandPublishers

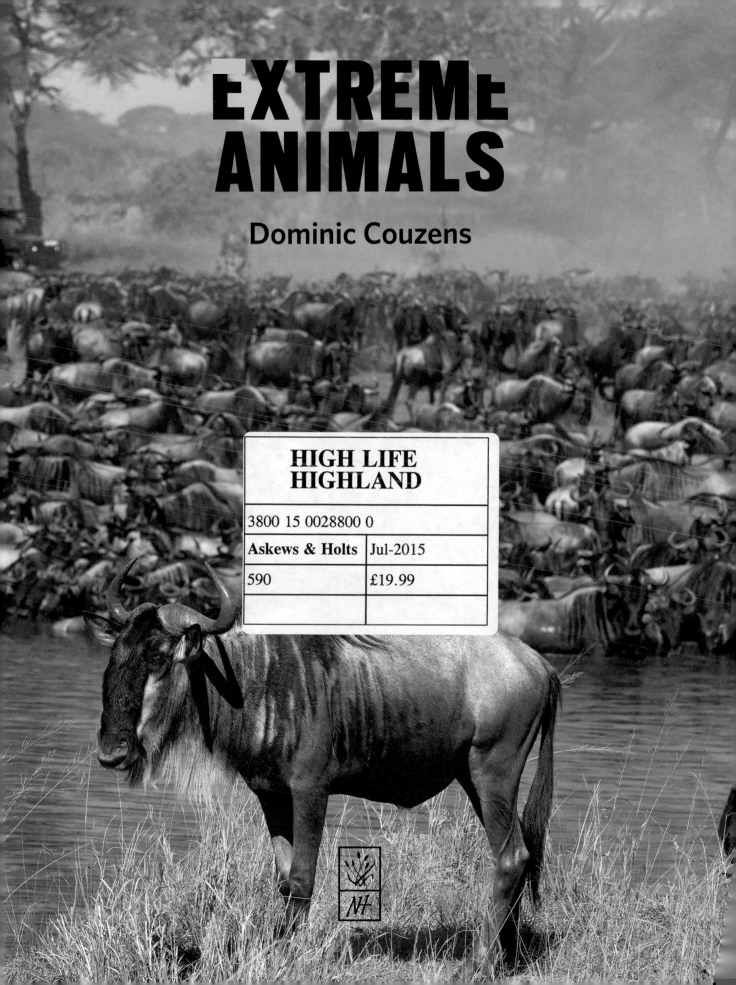

EXTREME
ANIMALS

Dominic Couzens

HIGH LIFE HIGHLAND	
3800 15 0028800 0	
Askews & Holts	Jul-2015
590	£19.99

CONTENTS

INTRODUCTION

This book is a collection of stories about animals that are out of the ordinary. It details many of the creatures that are record-holders – the largest, the smallest, the most venomous, and so on – but also documents those whose behaviour could be described as 'extreme'. In recent years and decades scientists have revealed all kinds of weird and wonderful ways in which animals do things, from frogs that brood young in their stomachs to rodents that live in the same types of colonies as bees. There are so many of these stories that no book could include them all, so this collection cherry-picks a sample of the most fascinating cases from a large pot of simply amazing facts.

The book has been designed to cover as wide a variety of stories as possible, to include all the obscure stuff such as snails and fish as well as the iconic wildlife such as elephants and whales. To this end, the book is divided into chapters which are arranged by group of creature, and although there is more information about mammals and birds than anything else, the amphibians, reptiles, fish and invertebrates have not been neglected. Indeed, my own favourite story is about a single-celled protozoan that makes rats lose their fear of cats, so that it can end up in its primary home, the cat's intestine. There is also a wide geographical spread of stories, covering everywhere from the highest mountains to the deepest seas, coming from every continent on earth and even venturing into outer space. As far as natural history is concerned, there is a great story around literally every corner.

The tales here are told primarily for fun, but every book like this also has a serious purpose. Life on this planet is wondrously diverse and deliciously odd, but also very vulnerable. Many scientists say that we are on the verge of the next great extinction – the first to be caused by people. If this book has a purpose it will be to inspire readers initially to delight in the natural world, and then to play their part in efforts to protect it.

MAMMALS

SMALLEST VARIATION WITHIN A LITTER

There are many peculiarities about the armour-plated burrowing mammals known as armadillos, but one of the strangest is that within a given litter (which might contain four individuals) all the youngsters are genetically identical to each other. They are effectively clones. This has been proven in studies of the Nine-banded Armadillo, *Dasypus novemcinctus* (above). In this species, the female produces a single egg that then divides.

Nobody knows what advantage this might confer on these ancient animals. Clones might be expected to show some degree of altruism towards one another, but nothing of the kind has been recorded in the wild because, once independent, the individuals go their separate ways. It might simply be an adaptation to some kind of physical restriction inherent in female armadillos that enables them only to produce a single fertilised egg.

BEST SCULPTED POO

On the whole, mammals have none of the revulsion that humanity shows towards faeces. Quite the reverse – if you're the average fox or deer, your own faeces are your trademark, and you can send life's most important messages from your rear end. These are messages of territorial ownership, age, health and sex, all contained within the chemical mix of expelled substances.

It is not surprising, therefore, that some mammals don't just defecate, but make their efforts into something of an art form. And no mammal is better known for this than that Australian icon, the Common Wombat, *Vombatus ursinus*. This marsupial manages to produce six-sided, cubic poos, which are remarkably neat and often quite dry, like building bricks. Even now, nobody actually knows how they manage to produce them.

We do know why they are cubic, though. Wombats are territorial, and they mark their patches of ground with faeces. The advantage of having flat-sided droppings is that once they are piled up, they remain in place, unmoved by wind or rain. They are conspicuous and unequivocal, as is their message to other wombats.

The Common Wombat (left) is a herbivore, with relatively solid poo like building bricks.

FRIENDLIEST VAMPIRES

Vampires get a bad press – and that despite the fact that the human versions don't even exist. Let's face it, though, blood is important to us, and we don't take kindly to having various types of animals – mosquitoes, ticks and flies, for example – taking without asking.

There are, however, some blood-eating animals that are entirely admirable: namely, vampire bats (subfamily Desmodontinae). Yes, they do suck the blood of animals, including from peoples' livestock and occasionally humans as well. Two of the three species specialise on birds. Yet within their own communities they show a remarkable level of mutual sharing and co-operation.

Blood is a rich diet but its sources are far from reliable. And one of the biggest problems for a vampire bat is that if it is starved of blood for more than three days it will not survive – these bats don't eat anything else at all. Vampire bats live in colonies and within these groups some bats simply might experience one or two unproductive nights. So what they do is solicit blood from another member of the colony, and they do this by licking their colleague's lips. More often than not, the request will be heeded and the blood regurgitated and shared.

It isn't quite as simple as this, though, because there is always the chance that a stranger might solicit blood, or a colony member might do the same when they just wish to be lazy. Therefore, vampire bat society puts in safeguards. Firstly, a bat will only share blood with a known colony member (they need to have roosted together at least 60 per cent of the time) – most colonies consist only of females, many of which are related. Secondly, a bat will invariably monitor the condition of the colleague that is begging for food. Before they ever share blood, vampire bats will first groom each other, and it is apparently easy for them to see and feel whether a colony-mate is faking an empty stomach.

Blood-sharing in vampire bats is a rare case of what is known as reciprocal altruism. The benefits for a needy bat greatly outweigh the cost of sharing blood, and no bat can be sure when it might need the same transfusion service.

It might look frightening, but the White-winged Vampire Bat, *Diaemus youngi*, mainly feeds on the blood of birds.

TALLEST ANIMAL

Nobody would be surprised to discover that the world's tallest animal is the Giraffe, *Giraffa camelopardalis* (left and below), the biggest individuals of which reach 6m (20ft) in height. They are uniquely adapted to feeding from the canopy branches of trees, well above the level reached by any other animals. It is their niche and they have a large browsing area to themselves.

Being so tall is awkward physiologically, because there is much pressure on the heart to pump blood to the head, which is 3m above the heart, and to the feet, which are 2m below. Furthermore, the sheer weight of blood should shatter the capillaries in the feet, and when a Giraffe bends down to drink the blood should pour down to the head and cause the brain to explode. However, the African savannahs are not littered with exploded Giraffe heads, owing to the fact that the arteries in the neck and feet subdivide into a fine mesh that regulates the blood-flow.

The physiological contortions of the Giraffe are nothing compared to the difficulties that must have been experienced by some of the larger sauropod dinosaurs. Animals such as *Brachiosaurus* (=*Giraffatitan*) regularly reached to 12m (40ft) and the tallest discovered, currently a beast known as *Sauroposeidon*, was supposedly 17m (56ft) in height. Furthermore, these animals may have sometimes reared up on their back legs to reach even higher. However, quite how their hearts managed to produce enough blood pressure to reach these literally dizzy heights is not yet fully explained.

The *Brachiosaurus* was about twice as tall as a Giraffe.

MOST EXHAUSTING BREEDING

Members of the small group of carnivorous marsupials known as antechinuses, *Antechinus* spp., have one of the more destructive types of breeding strategy, especially among mammals. Their lifestyle has been described as 'live fast, die young,' and the males, at least, live on borrowed time as soon as breeding begins. Indeed, you could say that during this time they have a choice between either living or reproducing, with no half-measures. They invariably choose reproduction.

Antechinuses, familiar to many Australians, tailor their breeding to allow the young to benefit from seasonal plenty. The only problem is that they cannot actually mate during those same beneficial times; on the contrary, they mate in the autumn when food is scarce. So the males put everything they have – all their bodily resources – into a short but intense mating period; even their immune system is neglected. They produce copious amounts of sperm and guard females by almost constant copulation, in an atmosphere of frenzied competition. The females can store the sperm, and most litters are the result of several males' efforts.

The males never live to see the fruits of their labour. After an explosive two weeks, they die of sheer physiological exhaustion.

TOUGHEST SKELETON

If you stand on top of an elephant you wouldn't expect to do it any damage; indeed, people have been riding on Indian Elephants for millennia and so far, no elephant backbone has buckled under the strain.

However, if you step on a shrew, a small mouse-like mammal with a snout, you might expect the result to be quite different. And for the majority of the hundreds of species, the consequences are final. We don't recommend you do this at home, but should your feet be so misplaced, your average trodden-on shrew would be suitably squished.

Unless, that is, it's a Hero Shrew, *Scutisorex somereni*. This animal lives in the forests of the Congo and the people there delight in standing on it with their full weight, without causing it any harm, in order to demonstrate its extraordinary resilience. The animal is only 12–15cm (5–6in) long, plus tail of 7–10cm (3–4in), so you can easily hold one on your hand. Not surprisingly, the tribes of the Congo Basin attribute magical powers to it.

The Hero Shrew has an extraordinary backbone, quite unlike any other shrew or any other mammal. Each vertebra is extensively corrugated, with many interlocking sections within and between the bones of the vertebral column. The rib-bones are also unusually strong, but the limb-bones are perfectly normal.

The real mystery is why this obscure animal should have such an unusual backbone. No observations have so far detected anything particularly strange about its lifestyle. It runs about and eats worms and other invertebrates like any other shrew. However, recent work suggests that it might lever logs and palm fronds over so that it can reach the insects hiding beneath.

BEST LONG-DISTANCE COMMUNICATION (LAND)

It has long been known that elephants seem to have a sixth sense. Groups of African Savannah Elephants, *Loxodonta africana*, are known to be able to synchronise their movements, even when well out of sight and a long distance away from each other. Observations have been made of elephants apparently 'freezing' in the same way humans might do when trying to pick up faint signals. Elephants also have to find mates in different herds that may be well separated.

Elephants use many modes of communication, including sight, scent and sound; they have a very low-pitched component to their voices which is below the range of humans (infrasound) and travels up to about 10km (6.2 miles) in ideal conditions.

In recent years, evidence for another, intriguing method of communication has come to light: seismic sensing, or paying heed to vibrations in the ground. It happens that seismic energy travels most efficiently between 10Hz and 40Hz, coinciding with the fundamental frequency and second harmonic of an elephant's low-pitched rumbling call. Although these sounds travel through the air, they can also travel through the ground.

How, though, does an elephant pick up the seismic component of another's call? Nobody knows yet, but the most plausible suggestion would appear to be Pacinian Corpuscles; vibrations deform rows of these bodies and trigger a signal to the brain. There are large numbers of these at the tip of the elephant's trunk, and also on its feet – the latter being a logical site to pick up vibrations from the earth.

BELOW: Elephants make low-pitched rumbling sounds below the register of human hearing, but audible with their large ears.

RIGHT: It is possible that elephants can detect sounds with their feet.

DEEPEST DIVE

Many odd creatures live at the bottom of the sea, but deep oceanic water is one of the most inhospitable habitats on earth for air-breathing animals. The intense pressure, combined with decompression problems, mean that deep-diving mammals have to be highly adapted, with collapsible lungs and ribs, limited nitrogen absorption and tolerance to carbon dioxide and lactic acid. Marine mammals tend to exchange 90 per cent of their oxygen with each breath, and they have very efficient oxygen retention in their blood.

Recent tagging studies suggest that the deepest diving animals are the beaked whales, which feed on the bottom of the ocean using suction, taking squid and deep sea fish. Cuvier's Beaked Whales, *Ziphius cavirostris*, off the coast of California astonished scientists in March 2014 by diving down to 2,992m (9,816ft, or 1.9 miles) and remaining there for more than 2 hours. This is the current world record.

Not far behind Cuvier's Beaked Whale is the Great Sperm Whale, *Physeter macrocephalus* (above), which reaches depths of 2,250m (7,380ft). It also feeds on squid.

Nobody would be surprised to know that whales dive deep, so this makes the feat of the Southern Elephant Seal, *Mirounga leonina* (above and right), even more impressive. This animal regularly feeds below 1,000m (1,280ft), and has been recorded staying down for 2 hours and reaching depths of 2,133m (6,998ft). It feeds on squid and fish, which it seems to catch by using vibration from its sensitive whiskers, and also the natural bioluminescence of some of its prey. In shallower waters it uses sight.

HEAVIEST TONGUE

To be honest, nobody should have the slightest interest in which of the world's animals has the heaviest tongue. The answer is always going to be the Blue Whale, *Balaenoptera musculus*, because the Blue Whale, being the world's largest animal, tends to have the world's largest everything (admittedly not arms and legs, but many other organs, including the heart, which can be as big as a small car). However, the enjoyable fact is that the Blue Whale's tongue can weigh 2.7 tonnes, which just happens to be heavier than some adult elephants, the world's largest land animal!

BEST DEFENCE OF YOUNG

If you are a young animal living out in the rough and tumble of the natural world, one of the things you most need is a big, dangerous and angry protector. And that's exactly the case for every young Musk-ox, *Ovibos moschatus* (left and above, with young). Musk-oxen live in the Arctic of North America and Greenland, and they are hairy, heavy and belligerent. An adult weighs in the region of 285kg (630lb) and this, combined with the large, sharp horns, meeting together in a large boss in the centre, makes it a formidable animal. Furthermore, Musk-oxen live in herds of up to about 20 animals throughout the year. If the herd is threatened by predators, which include both Wolf, *Canis lupus*, and Brown Bear, *Ursus arctos*, it has an unusual method of defence. The herd forms a tightly packed ring, with the fully-grown animals facing outwards towards the threat, and the youngsters are literally barged towards the centre. The adults may hold their position, but equally likely they will circle around the calves, making it even more dangerous for any animal to try to penetrate the ring. Not surprisingly, once the calves are protected in this way, they are rarely taken.

LAZIEST ANIMAL

If you measure 'laziness' by the amount of sleep an animal gets, then there are two contenders for this dubious honour. One is Australia's Koala, *Phascolarctos cinereus* (right), a marsupial that may sleep for 20 hours a day owing to the sheer calorific feebleness of its principal diet of eucalyptus leaves.

But Lions, *Panthera leo* (below), have no such excuse. They don't eat leaves, but the flesh of antelopes and other large animals, which are high in calories. Nonetheless, these big cats also idle the day away, having a short period of heightened activity at dusk in between 20 hours of doing nothing.

Blue Whales can communicate with each other across huge expanses of ocean.

LONGEST-DISTANCE COMMUNICATION (OCEAN)

As far as we humans know, the longest communication distance between one animal and another is about 1,600km (1,000 miles). This is only theoretical, because nobody has ever been able to tally a signal given with a signal received.

But then again, why else would Blue Whales, *Balaenoptera musculus*, use infrasounds? Infrasounds are sonic signals with a frequency below the range of human hearing; in the case of the Blue Whale their voices range from 8–20Hz (people can hear down to 20Hz). The great advantage of infra-sounds is that their low frequency corresponds to a relatively longer wavelength, meaning that the signal can pass through a medium for much further before dissipating. Whales, of course, live in water, which is a better medium than air for transmission, and at great depths the oceans make perfect sound channels.

The Blue Whale makes the loudest sounds of any animal, peaking at 180 decibels. And that's why scientists think that, at one time, Blue Whales and other species could communicate across the oceans.

These days, however, the oceans reverberate with all kinds of polluting human sounds, from shipping to sonar. It is thought that nowadays Blue Whales can only pass on messages for distances of about 160km (100 miles). But Blue Whales alive today will probably have experienced the different world of 80 or 90 years ago when they could probably enjoy the longest direct communication between any animals on earth.

Naked Mole-Rats live underground in colonies.

STRANGEST MAMMAL COLONY

The Naked Mole-Rat, *Heterocephalus glaber*, which is every bit as ugly as it sounds (indeed worse), is a burrowing rodent from East Africa. It lives in colonies numbering between 20 and 300 animals. These colonies are exceptionally odd in that their structure has more in common with those of bees, wasps and ants than with other mammal colonies, such as those of seals and bats.

In Naked Mole-Rat society there is a single reproductive female known as the queen. She will mate with anywhere between one and three males. Every other member of the colony is non-breeding, and most are sterile. Just as in ants and bees, the rest of the colony is made up of workers, which are charged with three main tasks: looking after the pups, tunnelling, and protecting the colony from predators. Needless to say, members of the protective group are known as 'soldiers'.

As in the social insects, the queen may live for a long time – up to 18 years. Only when she finally dies does one of the other females switch from non-reproductive to reproductive, and then only after a furious fight with other females with their poorly developed eyes, on the top job.

SMALLEST MAMMAL

Measurements of small size are always contentious, owing to the complications of weight against length and individual variation. However, despite this, two species have traditionally vied for the title of world's smallest mammal.

The smallest bat in the world is the Bumblebee Bat, *Craseonycteris thonglongyai*, so named because it is similar in size to a large bumblebee. The skull length (some mammalogists prefer this measurement) is only 11mm (0.43in), and the animal itself is just 2.9-3.3cm (1.14-1.30in) long. It is said to weigh 2-3g (0.07-0.10oz). This is a poorly known species, only discovered in 1974 in Thailand, and now known to occur in Myanmar too. It roosts deep in limestone caves in forests.

Its terrestrial rival is the Etruscan Shrew, *Sorex etruscus*, which occurs from southern Europe east to China and south to North Africa. This shrew is so small that it can fit into burrows made by large earthworms, and it will sometimes fall victim to large insects such as the praying mantids. The typical length of an adult is just 3.6-5.3cm (1.42-2.01in) and the weight ranges between 1.2-2.7g (0.04-0.10oz). The skull length is 13mm (0.5in), longer than the bat, but on the whole it is probably the lighter animal on average.

LARGEST MAMMAL

The world's largest mammal is the Blue Whale, *Balaenoptera musculus* (above). The longest reliably measured specimen was 33.27m (109ft) in length, from South Georgia in the South Atlantic in 1926. Since animals of such length are so vast it is almost impossible to estimate their weight, but 160 tonnes has been suggested.

The Blue Whale occurs in most of the world's oceans, although there is a 'pygmy' version that is really much smaller.

It is generally agreed that the Blue Whale is the largest animal that has ever lived, although some of the largest sauropod dinosaurs may have approached this length thanks to their supremely long necks and tails. And perhaps there have been larger marine reptiles and fish whose fossils have never been found?

SMELLIEST MAMMAL

Mammals use scent a great deal in communication, even across long distances, but as far as the human sense of smell is concerned, the world's most potent stink comes from the notorious Striped Skunk, *Mephitis mephitis* (right). When one of these small, actually very sleek carnivores considers that it is cornered, it releases a spray packed with repellent, foul-smelling chemicals. The worst of these is so potent that even at a concentration of 10 parts per billion it is detectable to the human nose. And of course, there's lots of it. An encounter with a frightened skunk will cause retching and nausea.

To make matters worse, skunks have powerful muscles at the side of their anal glands which shoot the foul mixture with deadly accuracy over a distance of several metres. If you get hit, you might just as well throw away any clothes affected. That's once you have finished throwing up.

BEST CONFLICT RESOLUTION

Conflicts abound in the natural world, between different animals and within species. In the latter case, there is typically high tension over access to food, territories and a mate. More often than not, these rivalries lead to violence, or implied violence.

There is one animal, however, that has a unique method of conflict resolution: sex. In societies of the Bonobo, *Pan paniscus* (left), sex would seem to be something of a cure-all. It breaks out when the animals are excited, when they are agitated and, of course, when they are affectionate too. These apes, the closest relatives of the Chimpanzee, *P. troglodytes*, live in groups of 20–50 of no fixed membership; individuals can come and go as they please. Any groups formed are dominated by females, which keep the males in check and have reasonably harmonious hierarchies. There are no long-term pair-bonds between males and females. And when there is any dispute, the answer is to lessen the tension by indulging in sexual behaviour, both during and after the dispute (above).

Sexual relations occur between all members of a group, with the exception of mothers and sons. That means, of course, that males will mate with males and females with females; much older animals will mate with younger ones. The catalogue of sexual encounters is, shall we say, long and detailed.

The Bonobo is no more productive as a breeding animal than the more conventional, and usually far more violent, Chimpanzee. It is just that sex is socially far more important. Most individual Bonobos have sex every day, often several times per day.

And that is why every human student who believes in reincarnation has returning as a Bonobo at the top of their wish-list.

The famous yeti is now thought to be a bear. It is genetically closest to the Polar Bear (right), but could even be a hybrid with the Brown Bear (above).

MOST TANTALISING DNA MYSTERY

One of the most enduring of all stories of mysterious creatures as yet unknown to science concerns the supposed bipedal hominid-like 'Yeti' of the Himalayas. For many years there have been sightings of large, dark, hairy beings in the forests and snow-drifts of the region, together with large, human-like footprints. Tantalisingly, nobody has ever found a specimen or taken an incontrovertibly reliable photograph or moving image, so the mystery has endured.

You might expect a DNA sample to put an end to such a mystery once and for all, but recent analysis of a hair taken from the supposed lair of a Yeti in Bhutan did, in some ways, deepen the intrigue. Scientists at Oxford University checking the world database of animal DNA found a 100 per cent match with material from a 40,000-year-old skull of a Polar Bear, *Ursus maritimus*, found on the Svalbard island group north of Norway. The Yeti, therefore, would appear to be bear. But whether it is a Polar Bear, a hybrid with a Brown Bear, *Ursus arctos*, or a new bear species is still to be determined. And the idea that an unknown large bear could be hiding away all these years, even in the remote Himalayas, is quite something.

MOST COSTLY FIGHTS

Plenty of animals are accustomed to fighting to achieve supremacy – think of deer stags, kicking kangaroos and drunken humans outside a club – it is often simply part of being male. However, fighting is by and large a means to an end and serious injuries are avoided. If a stag, for instance, knows that it is inferior to a harem owner, it simply won't challenge him, keeping its powder dry for another year when it can. Males usually know when they are outmuscled (unless they are inebriated, of course), and serious fights usually only occur between very well-matched rivals, or between males in which the stakes are unusually high.

However, there is one mammal in which fights to the death occur with abnormal regularity, and that's the Black Rhinoceros, *Diceros bicornis*. In one study it was found that a remarkably high proportion of all adults – 50 per cent of males and 33 per cent of females – were killed as a result of combat between males for access to females. The violent nature of the fighting is exacerbated by the large size and power of the animals, as well as the sharp and deadly horn.

THICKEST SKIN

It isn't strictly skin, but the animal with the thickest outer protective layer is the very rare Bowhead Whale, *Balaena mystacetus*. The layer of blubber protecting this animal is no less than 40cm (16in) thick, and in places 50cm (20in).

The Bowhead needs it, too, being the only whale that spends the whole year in the cold waters of the Arctic and sub-Arctic. In fact, the covering is so effective that the whale is thought to use a special area on its head, with a thick network of blood vessels, to keep it cool and prevent overheating.

The Bowhead Whale doesn't just have a thick skin, it has a thick skull, too, and it is capable of using its head to smash through up to 60cm (24in) of ice in order to breathe. It has the largest mouth of any living organism.

LEFT: Apart from people, the biggest danger to the formidable Black Rhino is ... another Black Rhino.
RIGHT: The massive bones of a Bowhead Whale washed up on an Alaskan Shore.

FASTEST LAND MAMMAL

The fastest land animal is the Cheetah, *Acinonyx jubatus* (above), of Africa and southern Asia. When running at a full sprint it can reach 102km/h (63mph), comfortably outrunning any other mammal. Horses, one of the fastest herbivores, can run at a maximum speed of 88km/h (54.7mph) and a human can reach a relatively feeble 44.7km/h (27.8mph). So it's just as well for us that we aren't food for Cheetahs. On the other hand, a Lion, *Panthera leo*, can run at 45–60km/h (28–37mph) in very short bursts of 100–200m (330–660ft).

The Cheetah is built for speed, with longer and slimmer legs than any other cat, a light build, a deep narrow chest and a domed skull to cut down air resistance. Its stride is exceptionally long, helped by curvature of the spine. However, in practice it is not so much the Cheetah's raw speed that makes the difference, it is its acceleration and agility. It can accelerate four times faster than a human (from a standstill to maximum speed in just three seconds), but most chases are much shorter, and the hunter depends upon its ability to jink and weave as effectively as its prey (often gazelles) in order to make the kill. About 50 per cent of all chases are successful. The Cheetah needs to stalk its prey to within about 30m (100ft) to give itself a chance of success.

LARGEST BAT COLONY

This is probably the Bracken Bat Cave near the city of San Antonio, Texas, USA. During the breeding season it contains between 15 and 20 million Mexican Free-tailed Bats, *Tadarida brasiliensis*. Other estimates have reached as high as 40 million, but you can imagine how hard it is to be accurate. The animals rest in the dark cave during the day and then stream out at dusk to feed; it apparently takes four hours for all the bats to depart. No instrument can accurately measure the number of animals involved.

Not surprisingly, these animals eat a lot of flying insects. Even if every bat ate just one insect per night, that would be at least 15 million insects. But in fact when the females are feeding young they have to collect their own weight in food each night, which amounts to 100 tons of flying bugs every night. It seems incredible that the night sky accommodates so many insects, but it clearly does, although the bats may have to fly high and far to obtain them. They frequently rise in height to 180–1,000m (590–3,280ft) to feed, and some individuals have been recorded at 3,000m (9,850ft), which also makes this species the highest-flying bat in the world.

Recently land around the Bracken Bat Cave has been bought in order to form a buffer zone to preserve it. The Mexican Free-tailed Bat seems to prefer to live in just a few very large concentrations. Another very famous colony occurs within the city limits of Austin, Texas. There are an estimated 1.5 million bats roosting under the Congress Avenue Bridge (main picture). Large numbers of human viewers gather on the bridge each night in season (March–November) to watch the enormous emergence – perhaps the biggest urban wildlife spectacular in the world.

SNEAKIEST FEEDING

While we're on the subject of Mexican Free-tailed Bats, research has recently been published that shows that they don't always play fair when they are up in the heights catching food. As most people know, bats hunt by using a kind of sonar system, shouting out high-frequency sounds (usually from the mouth) and monitoring the echoes they receive back from hard objects – a process known as echolocation. Sometimes, it seems, if two bats are chasing the same food in the same location, one individual will deliberately jam the echolocation signal by calling out at the same frequency, swamping the return signal and effectively robbing its rival of the ability to home in correctly on its intended target, which is usually a moth. The distracted bat will often miss, and the rival's underhand tactics will enable it to 'steal' the food.

BIGGEST ANIMAL MIGRATION

The 'biggest' animal migration certainly isn't the longest journey, but in terms of sheer biomass it quite literally outweighs all the others. It is the annual migration on foot by the grazing animals of the Serengeti Plains in East Africa. The largest contingent of animals are Serengeti White-bearded Wildebeest, *Connochaetes mearnsi*, with 1.3 million individuals, together with 350,000 Serengeti Thomson's Gazelles, *Eudorcas nasalis*, and 200,000 Plains Zebra, *Equus quagga* – so just under 2 million animals in total. Although their journeys can vary somewhat from year to year, they tend to walk in a wide circle totalling 450km (280 miles).

The year begins for these animals in the short-grass plains of the southern Serengeti, where many give birth between February and March. A reduction in food begins to force the animals north-westwards by June each year. Zebras depart first, followed by groups of wildebeest that coalesce into enormous herds; the gazelles leave last. All the animals are attracted by sensing thunderstorms that begin to soak the savannahs of the Maasai Mara, stimulating new grazing. Their stay here is quite brief (the grasses are short on essential nutrients), and so the animals eventually walk back to where they started.

This remarkable round-trip has many dangers, not least the crossing of rivers, especially the Mara River in the northernmost part of the journey. As featured on many a TV documentary, many animals perish, to drowning and to crocodiles.

Remarkably, in our crowded world, another very nearly comparable migration of large mammals takes place not very far to the north, in south-eastern Sudan and Ethiopia. This is a 250-km (150-mile) trek performed by 750,000 White-eared Kob, *Kobus leucotis*, 300,000 Mongalla Gazelles, *Eudorcas albonotata*, 150,000 Tiang antelopes, *Damaliscus tiang*, and 6,000 African Savannah Elephants, *Loxodonta africana*. The kob breed in the Sudd Swamp region by the White Nile from January to April. Heavy rains stimulate a southward migration into seasonally productive savannah country, with the animals returning north in October.

TOP: The trek undertaken annually by the Serengeti White–bearded Wildebeest only takes the animals about 450km (280 miles) in total, but it has its share of hazards, not least the Mara River.
LEFT: It isn't only wildebeest that roam the Serengeti; nearly a quarter of a million zebras do, too.

BIGGEST SIZE DIFFERENCE BETWEEN PREDATOR AND PREY

The animal kingdom is full of unfair fights and chases – think of cats eating mice, dolphins eating small fish and chameleons snaring bugs on the end of their tongues. What, though, might be the biggest difference in size between predator and prey?

This is an easy question to answer, because the world's largest animal, the Blue Whale, *Balaenoptera musculus* (right), subsists on relatively tiny prey. This behemoth of the deep, which measures up to 30m (100ft) long, is almost entirely dependent on krill (family Euphausiidae) for its sustenance. These small marine shrimp-like crustaceans (above) measure anything between 1–6cm (0.4–2.4in) long, meaning that the whale is at least 5,000 times longer than its prey.

The krill carnage is mind-boggling. A Blue Whale may eat 40 million krill in a single day, that is 3,600kg (7,940lb). That's 40 million crustacean deaths, individuals snuffed out. The whale eats them by sieving them out of the water. It lunges towards a cloud of krill and closes its mouth over them, water and all. The water is expelled through narrow plates on the upper jaw known as baleen, which collectively forms a barrier, a little like the teeth of a comb. So, while the water can be washed away, the krill gets caught up in the baleen and is eventually steered towards the gullet.

LONGEST MIGRATION ON FOOT

The longest migration of any terrestrial animal is undertaken by the Reindeer, *Rangifer tarandus* (below), which is known as the Caribou in North America. These animals live in the tundra of the Northern Hemisphere, which they evacuate in the depths of winter. Caribou have been recorded travelling 5,000km (3,100 miles) in a single year. Their southbound migration to wooded areas begins in late August, and the first part of the journey coincides with a rut. The northbound journey to the open tundra starts in March.

On their migration Reindeer often gather into enormous herds of up to 500,000 individuals. They travel between 20–50km (12–31 miles) a day.

BIRDS

MOST PROMISCUOUS BIRD

If any bird is living proof that beauty is merely in the eye of the beholder, it would have to be the Corn Bunting, *Emberiza calandra* (right). This bird of European cornfields is remarkably dull in plumage and somewhat squat in shape, and it delivers a reasonably pleasant, but hardly masterful song. However, this unlikely lothario probably holds the record for the number of females paired to a single male bird in a wild situation.

The record-holder inhabited a field in Sussex, England, in 1985. In the course of a season it mated with no less than 18 individual females, and it was paired with many of them at the same time. Its total production was not estimated at the time but, bearing in mind that a Corn Bunting lays up to six eggs, this could in theory mean that 108 youngsters descended from one male in one season.

There are no records of what happened to this remarkable bird the following summer, but one thing is for sure: it died happy.

BEST IMPRESSIONIST

One of the quirks of bird song is the ability, found in a wide variety of species, to incorporate imitations of other sounds into an individual's repertoire. One of the best-known mimics is the Superb Lyrebird, *Menura novaehollandiae* (top left), of Australia, which imitates a wide variety of bush birds, and occasionally human sounds too. These can include camera shutters, chainsaws, car alarms, crying babies and music.

The most famous mimic in North America is the Northern Mockingbird, *Mimus polyglottos* (top right). Both these celebrated species mimic at least 30–50 other bird species, although both do it with variable levels of quality.

However, in terms of the number of species that are imitated, the prize goes to two much less well-known species. The Marsh Warbler, *Acrocephalus palustris* (main picture), has a song comprised almost entirely of mimicry, with the males first learning the songs and calls of other European bird species on their breeding grounds, and then adding the vocalisations of other species from their wintering grounds in Africa. An analysis of 30 individual Marsh Warblers revealed imitations of 99 European species and a further 133 from Africa, making 232 species in total (with no doubt plenty more unknown).

The Marsh Warbler's most serious rival is perhaps the Lawrence's Thrush, *Turdus lawrencii*, of Amazonia. To date, this songster has been known to impersonate 170 other bird species, plus a number of frogs and insects. Bearing in mind that a single bird once copied 51 other species in a single song bout, the suspicion is that Lawrence's Thrush will eventually be found to be the world's best mimic.

Incidentally, nobody knows why so many birds use mimicry in their songs. One suggestion is that it simply allows them to gain a wider repertoire, which has been shown to have a positive effect in terms of attracting females. Recent research, however, seems to suggest that they are simply straight copies of environmental sounds that creep into the song randomly.

MOST DECEPTIVE MIMIC

While many birds simply embellish their songs with mimicry, some are known to do it with a much more sinister purpose. Top among these is the Slaty-backed Forest Falcon, *Micrastur mirandollei*, which is a predator of other birds. It apparently perches in a concealed position and imitates the distress calls of a small bird. These attract the attention of the prey species upon which the forest falcon pounces. It thus lures them to their deaths.

A small South American forest bird, the Thick-billed Euphonia, *Euphonia laniirostris*, sometimes uses mimicry to summon support in moments of danger. When a predator approaches its nest it gives imitations of the calls of other common forest birds. These are attracted to the commotion and begin to mob the predator, which may then be driven off. Meanwhile, the euphonia continues to give off its mimicked calls, but keeps out of sight.

Still another case concerns the Fork-tailed Drongo, *Dicrurus adsimilis*, of sub-Saharan Africa. This bird often acts as a sentry among flocks of unrelated birds, making alarm calls when a predator approaches. However, only six of its alarm calls are its own, while it makes 45 other alarm calls that are copies from other species. On occasion, when it spies that a flock member has a very good feeding spot or a large morsel of food, it will give that species' alarm call and disturb the successful individual. Having deceived its colleague into flight, it will then drop down and steal the bounty. In order for this to work effectively, however, the drongo only performs the deception occasionally. For much of the time it is a reliable sentry.

....

LEFT: The Thick-billed Euphonia, when threatened, summons help from all quarters by imitating neighbouring species.
TOP: A Fork-tailed Drongo uses a zebra as a lookout post.

A pair of Sociable Weavers.

LARGEST NEST

The largest bird nest in the world is built by the Sociable Weaver, *Philetairus socius*. As you might expect from the name, it isn't a single nest but a communal one and may be used by more than 100 pairs at a time. The nest is built in a tree or on a man-made structure such as a pole, and it may weigh more than 1 tonne despite being composed of little more than grass stems. The largest examples known have measured 4m (13ft) wide and 7.2m (23.6ft) tall. A Sociable Weaver nest is the largest structure made by any bird. Occasionally, large birds such as vultures or Verreaux's Eagle-Owls, *Bubo lacteus*, use the nests as a platform for their own nests, creating the largest structure made by two bird species. The sheer weight of a weaver nest may cause its supporting tree or branch to collapse.

The nest consists of many small chambers 10–15cm (4–6in) in diameter, each of which is used by one pair. However, not all chambers are used for nesting. Inner chambers retain heat and are used for roosting at night, while outer chambers may be 10°C (18°F) cooler than ambient temperature, or even more. The benign properties sometimes attract other species of birds to use them for roosting, and even nesting – the Pygmy Falcon, *Polihierax semitorquatus*, is a frequent breeding tenant.

OPPOSITE TOP RIGHT: Sociable Weaver nests, like these on telegraph poles, quite often cause their supporting structures to collapse.
OPPOSITE BOTTOM RIGHT: The 'nest' is more like an apartment building than a single nest, with many units.

A Brünnich's Guillemot

The Purple Sandpiper breeds on treeless coasts and tundra

DEEPEST DIVING BIRD

This is one of several records held by the remarkable Emperor Penguin, *Aptenodytes forsteri*, which famously breeds in some of the most inhospitable parts of Antarctica. In its quest for squid and fish it can search near the bottom of the sea, and has been known to reach a depth of 535m (1,755ft). It often alternates much shallower dives of 50–150m (165–495ft) with deep ones.

In recent years, several seabird species have confounded researchers by diving much deeper than expected. A good example is the Brünnich's Guillemot, *Uria lomvia*, a species thought not to go much deeper than 20–30m (66–98ft). Recent studies have shown that it regularly dives down to 150m (492ft) and has been recorded at 210m (689ft).

··

LEFT: Emperor Penguins are adapted far more to the sea than to the land, and dive deeper than any other bird.

CLEVEREST DEFENCE OF YOUNG

The Purple Sandpiper, *Calidris maritima*, breeds in the tundra, where the ground is open and where its eggs and young are highly vulnerable to predators. It has thus evolved some clever ways of keeping intruders away from its nest, including the well-known 'broken-wing' display, in which the adult bird makes itself conspicuous and feigns injury to its wing, drawing the attention of an Arctic Fox, *Vulpes lagopus*, for example, away from its well-hidden family and towards an apparently incapacitated potential meal.

Its most remarkable nest-defence strategy, however, is known as the 'rodent run', in which this small shorebird effectively pretends to be a lemming or vole. It flexes its legs so that it creeps along like a rodent, runs haphazardly back and forth, and even makes squeaking sounds similar to a small mammal.

··

Two famous record-holders. Left, a Bee Hummingbird, the world's smallest bird and above, Arctic Tern, the world's longest-distance migrant.

SMALLEST BIRD

The world's smallest bird is undoubtedly a hummingbird (family Trochilidae), but several species are very nearly as small as each other, and these birds reach the physiological limits of how small a vertebrate can be. The official record-holder is the Bee Hummingbird, *Mellisuga helenae*, of Cuba, the adult of which is 5.7cm (2.24in) long and weighs 1.6–1.8g (0.056–0.063oz). The Little Woodstar, *Chaetocercus bombus*, of western South America has been quoted as weighing 1.6g (0.056oz), but normally it weighs more than 2.2g (0.078oz), so perhaps the 1.6g individual was having a bad day. The Vervain Hummingbird, *Mellisuga minima*, of the West Indies is frequently mentioned as the world's second-smallest bird, measuring just about 6cm (2.36in) long and weighing 2.0–2.4g (0.071–0.085oz). The Short-tailed Woodstar, *Myrmia micrura*, and Gorgeted Woodstar, *Chaetocercus heliodor*, are only 7cm (2.76in) long, as is the Bumblebee Hummingbird, *Atthis heloisa*, which weighs in at about 2.2g (0.078oz). The point is that all these hummers are so small that the slightest error in measuring instruments or method of measurement could establish a new record.

All of these birds look like large insects at first sight, and indeed they are smaller than a number of bees that compete with them for nectar.

The Vervain Hummingbird is reputed to lay the world's smallest egg, measuring just 1.0cm (0.39in) long and weighing 0.3g (0.011oz).

LONGEST MIGRATION

The longest migration from A to B and back is performed annually by the Arctic Tern, *Sterna paradisaea*. This small, elegant seabird often breeds far into the Arctic and then migrates south to winter in the Antarctic, meaning that it travels about as far as anything could in respect of north to south – a minimum of 19,000km (12,000 miles) each way. However, it is never as simple as that, because many individuals don't take a direct route, instead following coastlines rather than a straight oceanic course, and some apparently arrive in southern waters in a stir-crazy state, eager for more travelling. They might, for example, fly from Africa to Australia before moving into the Antarctic. Of a number of individual Arctic Terns satellite-tracked from their breeding areas in the Netherlands (so a considerable distance short of the Arctic), one flew about 91,000km (57,000 miles) in between one breeding attempt and the next.

Incidentally, by breeding in the northern Arctic and wintering in the Antarctic, this animal (along with any parasites it might carry on its plumage) sees more daylight in a year than any other.

LONGEST DISTANCE TRAVELLED IN A YEAR

You might think that the Arctic Tern's impressive record of the longest migration might qualify it as the world's most travelled bird, but it doesn't. It is probable that quite a number of oceanic seabirds fly much further than an Arctic Tern in any given year. Most albatrosses (family Diomedeidae) probably do, and perhaps some shearwaters (family Procellariidae).

As far as albatrosses are concerned, their large size, long wings and open ocean habitat means that they can travel incredible distances: indeed, some Grey-headed Albatrosses, *Thalassarche chrysostoma*, have been known to cover 950km (590 miles) in a single *day*. A study of 13 satellite-tracked Wandering Albatrosses, *Diomedea exulans*, found that in their first year of fledged life they flew an average of 184,000km (114,300 miles), which is equivalent to 500km (310 miles) every single day. These great birds can fly long distances using the energy from the wind gradient above the waves, thereby hardly needing to flap their wings and using up very few of their internal resources.

There could hardly be a greater contrast in the movements of the two species on this page. The Wandering Albatross (left) is one of the world's greatest travellers, perhaps flying further in a single day than the Dusky Grouse (above) does in its entire lifetime.

SHORTEST MIGRATION

While many species of birds perform mind-boggling transcontinental migrations and are justly famous for their ability to navigate, not every species needs to travel far to meet its needs. In fact, the bird with the shortest migration could probably walk. It is the Dusky Grouse, *Dendragapus obscurus*, of western North America, and its shortest-known seasonal movement was just 400m (1,310ft). It rarely migrates more than about 10km (6 miles) in total.

The Dusky Grouse migrates between different habitats and different elevations, as do a number of bird species. However, it exhibits one further peculiar quirk: in the winter many individuals migrate uphill, not downhill as most altitudinal migrants do.

ABOVE: A Bar-tailed Godwit on its breeding grounds.
LEFT: Godwits migrate in small flocks. The birds are streamlined and powerful.

LONGEST SINGLE FLIGHT BY A LAND BIRD

While albatrosses can fly enormous distances using the energy of the wind and waves, and vultures can fly for a day on the swirling updrafts of thermals, it is quite another matter to travel vast distances powered only by your own wing-beats. That is why the world's longest non-stop migratory flight by a landbird, a shorebird called the Bar-tailed Godwit, *Limosa lapponica*, is so impressive. Every autumn, Alaskan breeding birds set out on a single-leg journey to their wintering grounds in New Zealand, 11,000km (6,835 miles) away.

To get some idea of how remarkable this is, it is worth comparing the birds with human-made aircraft. The longest time any aircraft has been able to fly without running out of fuel is about three and a half days, in the case of an unmanned solar-powered craft called *Zephyr*. The godwits, on the other hand, fly for eight days without food, water or any kind of break.

To achieve their feat, Bar-tailed Godwits burn off only 0.41 per cent of their body weight every hour, much less than most other migrant birds. They also fly fast and have an aerodynamically efficient body shape. And not only do they have to be supreme athletes to complete the journey, but their navigation has to be spot-on too. It would only take a mistake of a few degrees for the birds to miss New Zealand completely and end up in the oblivion of the Southern Ocean.

SMARTEST BIRD

Until recently birds were hardly noted for their intelligence; in fact the term 'bird-brained' was used in a derogatory fashion. However, we now know that birds have been misunderstood and underestimated and that some have impressive memory, learning, language and other cognitive skills.

It still comes as a shock, however, to learn that the world's most intelligent bird is the New Caledonian Crow, *Corvus moneduloides*, which is limited to its namesake island. Why on earth should a range-restricted bird, as opposed to a perhaps more adaptable species found over a wide range, be so clever? Nobody knows.

There is no doubt about its cleverness, though. In the wild it uses sophisticated tools to pry or pull food items, especially beetle larvae, out of holes. It manufactures these tools itself from twigs and stems, and these implements have standard designs used by different populations of birds, so the youngsters learn how to use them and practise until they are proficient. In laboratory tests the New Caledonian Crow can be remarkably clever at solving problems. For example, when captive individuals were taught to drop stones into an upright glass cylinder, they were then presented with floating food halfway up the same cylinder, but out of reach. Not only did the crows deduce that by dropping stones into the cylinder they could raise the water level and thus bring the food into reach, but they also selected only the largest stones in order to make the water level rise faster.

Other captive birds have shown that they can solve two-stage problems. On one occasion an individual was presented with a visible reward (food) that could only be obtained with a long stick (as in the wild). However, no such long stick was available without first using a different, shorter stick that could open the matchbox. The bird quickly worked out how to acquire the long stick by opening the matchbox, even though there was no immediate reward. Using one tool to obtain another to obtain a reward is known as 'meta-tool' use, and until it was demonstrated in New Caledonian Crows scientists thought that only the higher apes could master it.

Another unusual attribute of these bright sparks is that they can work out what mirrors do. If they are looking at a mirror and food is dropped behind their shoulder, they immediately turn and grab it from the right place – deducing that a mirror is a reflection. Gazing into a mirror isn't often a sign of intelligence, but in this case it is.

A recent experiment has shown that the crows are able to attribute an effect to a cause without directly observing the cause. In an experiment, an unseen human inserted a large stick close to the birds' feeding tray. If this happened randomly, the crows were afraid. If, however, they were able to see a human enter the hide next to their cage, they would then not recoil if the stick was inserted. Once they saw the human come close, they 'assumed' that the person was moving the stick, even though they couldn't see it directly. This type of deduction is apparently unusual even among super-intelligent apes.

Rumours that many of the world's politicians are soon going to be replaced by New Caledonian Crows are unfortunately unfounded.

HIGHEST FLYING BIRD

There are two birds famous for flying at greater heights than the rest. One is from Africa, the Rüppell's Vulture, *Gyps rueppellii*, which soars high over the land in order to look for carrion, as most vultures do. It uses thermals for lift, and presumably one individual that was hit by a commercial airliner at a height of 11,300m (37,000ft) over the Ivory Coast was literally being carried away.

Rüppell's Vultures are well adapted for high altitude flying and are sometimes seen above 6,000m (20,000ft). Their haemoglobin can absorb oxygen even at reduced atmospheric pressure. However, they are unlikely to be able to spot carrion at such great heights, so they probably use this ability mainly for travelling long distances.

The other bird famous for flying at great height could hardly be more different. The Bar-headed Goose, *Anser indicus*, is an odd candidate for any kind of record; it is a medium-sized goose with no obvious exceptional abilities. It cannot soar on thermals, so in order to fly high it has to do all the work itself, even in the thin air.

However, this goose breeds at high altitude in Central Asia and winters in the lowlands of South Asia, and between these areas is an inconvenience known as the High Himalayas. Rather than flying around the mountains, the Bar-headed Goose flies right through and over them, rising at times to an altitude of 5,784m (18,976ft) and exceptionally to 7,290m (23,920ft). The birds fly at night and make the whole crossing in one journey. In common with the Rüppell's Vulture, these geese have specially adapted haemoglobin, and more capillaries and red blood cells than their relatives.

Why do the geese fly over such a potentially dangerous barrier? One rather neat suggestion is that the geese have been around for a long time, and when they first started this migration the Himalayas weren't so high as they are now!

LEFT: The Rüppell's Vulture rides thermals, sometimes to extreme heights.
OVERLEAF: A flock of Bar-headed Geese

A flock of Bramblings, an abundant European Finch

One bird among 70 million

LARGEST FLOCK OF BIRDS

It is very difficult to make official statements about large flocks of birds for two simple reasons: firstly, the larger the flock the harder it is to estimate the numbers with any accuracy; and secondly, it depends what you mean by a flock. In 1951/2 an estimated 70 million Bramblings, *Fringilla montifringilla*, roosted in a valley in Switzerland, but they weren't all in a single flock.

Several birds do form very large, co-ordinated gatherings. Recent contenders include flocks of Red-billed Queleas, *Quelea quelea*, in sub-Saharan Africa, which contained millions of birds. One such gathering was estimated to hold 40 million birds, which took 5 hours to pass the observer. A winter roost of several species of New World Blackbirds (family Icteridae), including Red-winged Blackbirds, *Agelaius phoeniceus,* and grackles, genus *Quiscalus*, at the Great Dismal Swamp, Virginia, USA, was estimated to contain 15 million birds.

The real answer to the question will always be open to debate, but in recent times there have never been any gatherings to rival those claimed for the now extinct Passenger Pigeon, *Ectopistes migratorius*, of eastern North America in the early 1800s. One flock (and that's just one) by the Kentucky River was estimated to contain 2,230,272,000 birds, being a mile in breadth and passing the observer for four hours. The method of measurement wasn't particularly accurate, but it is likely that the Passenger Pigeon did form larger flocks than any other bird. It became extinct in 1914 after a drastic decline – but that's another story.

OPPOSITE TOP RIGHT: The Red-billed Quelea regularly forms the largest known single flocks of any species of bird
OPPOSITE RIGHT: The Red-winged Blackbird of North America forms large roosting flocks

MOST DANGEROUS BIRD

Very few people have ever been directly killed by a bird, especially a wild bird, making birding a much safer hobby than, for example, freestyle mammal-watching or diving unprotected with sharks. However, two species around the world are perhaps a fraction more dangerous than the rest.

The best-known is undoubtedly the Southern Cassowary, *Casuarius casuarius*, of Australia and New Guinea. This is a large flightless bird in the mould of an Ostrich or Emu, *Dromaius novaehollandiae*, but it is somewhat chunkier in build, with massive legs and feet and black, hair-like plumage. It has three toes on each foot, and on each inside toe is a very sharp, slightly curved claw up to 10cm (4in) long. When the cassowary is threatened in any way, including by people, it will jump up and kick, and in such circumstances the claws can cause real damage (although they cannot 'disembowel' a human, despite hysterical newspaper reports). One Australian fatality has been recorded (in 1926) and six serious injuries. In New Guinea, where there are two other cassowary species in addition to the Southern, and where the birds are sometimes kept as pets, people are killed from time to time, and probably hundreds have died over the long history of human-cassowary interaction.

While a cassowary only lashes out defensively, that certainly isn't true of the Crowned Eagle, *Stephanoaetus coronatus*, a large predatory raptor that specialises in hunting primates. There is a recorded instance of one attacking and injuring a seven-year-old boy, and the skull of a child was once found in the nest of a pair of these birds.

These instances are highly unusual, but some scientists think that in the distant past huge eagles preyed upon the young of our ancestors fairly frequently. A skull of a 2.5 million-year-old hominid was found in Africa with puncture marks around the eyes consistent with the talons of a monster Crowned Eagle-type predator.

OPPOSITE: The flightless, Ostrich-like Southern Cassowary is one of the world's largest and heaviest birds
TOP LEFT: The odd ornamentation on top of a cassowary's head is called a casque. Its function is not entirely clear
TOP RIGHT: Note the long, sharp claw on the inside toe of the cassowary's foot. (The outer claw here is unusual)

LARGEST BIRD

The world's largest bird, as well as the tallest and heaviest, is the Common Ostrich, *Struthio camelus*, of Africa and, formerly, the Middle East. The tallest adults can measure 2.8m (9.2ft) in height and weigh 156kg (344lb). The closely related Somali Ostrich, *Struthio molybdophanes*, is similar in measurements. The ostrich is also the fastest-running bird and, indeed, the fastest-running animal on two legs, reaching 70km/h (44mph) when sprinting. Living in the predator-rich plains of Africa, it needs to be fast and vigilant – it has the largest eyes of any bird.

Had this book been written a few hundred years ago, the ostrich would not be the largest, the heaviest or the tallest bird. Up until the end of the 17th century an enormous flightless forest species, known as the Giant Elephant Bird, *Aepyornis maximus*, lived on Madagascar. Estimates of its weight from sub-fossil bones range between 275–438kg (605–965lb), which is considerably greater than the ostrich. It had a shorter neck and shorter, thicker legs than the ostrich and a somewhat fur-like feathery covering, but still stood 3m (10ft) tall and must have been an impressive sight.

Even this giant was not the tallest bird of recent times. That accolade goes to the South Island Giant Moa, *Dinornis robustus*, of New Zealand, which became extinct some time between 1350 and 1450. Females, the larger sex in the species of this genus, probably reached 3.6m (12ft) in height.

LARGEST EGG

The Common Ostrich lays the largest egg of any extant bird, and they are consequently also the largest single cell in the world. On average the eggs are 14–17cm (5.5–6.7in) long and 11–14cm (4.3–5.5in) wide.

These measurements are dwarfed, however, by the egg of the extinct Giant Elephant Bird (see left column). Many sub-fossil eggs of this bird have been found, some intact, and some even with an embryonic skeleton inside. They measure up to 34cm (13.4in) in length and have a volume equivalent to that of 160 chicken eggs.

You might think that, being among the largest creatures ever to have roamed the planet, many dinosaur eggs might be larger. So far, however, this has not been the case.

OPPOSITE: The Ostrich never buries its head in the sand. It is nowadays the world's largest bird.
TOP LEFT: A male Ostrich courts a female (left). The result is the world's largest bird eggs.
TOP RIGHT: Ostrich eggs are impressively large, but those of the extinct Elephant Bird were almost twice as big.

Two lifestyles produce a long wing-span in birds. Seabirds such as the Wandering Albatross (right) use their long, narrow wings to save energy in windy environments such as the open ocean. Meanwhile, scavengers such as the Marabou Stork (above), vultures and condors ride thermals for hours on end on their long, very broad wings.

LONGEST WINGSPAN

Several bird species may lay claim to the longest wingspan, but the official record-holder is the Wandering Albatross, *Diomedea exulans*, with a maximum span of 3.63m (11.9ft). Several other species approach this figure, including the Marabou Stork, *Leptoptilos crumeniferus*, with 3.7m (12ft) claimed and the Andean Condor, *Vultur gryphus*, at 3.2m (10ft).

Today's birds are dwarfed by some fossils of birds from, in geological terms, the quite recent past. A family of giant birds resembling condors, the Teratornithidae, soared over the Americas about 6 million years ago, and one of their number, *Argentavis magnificens*, had a wingspan of somewhere between 6–8m (20–26ft). Another, unrelated bird from 25 million years ago, *Pelagornis sandersi*, is estimated to have a wingspan of 6.1–7.4 m (20–24ft).

ODDEST NEST-MATERIAL

Birds have a habit of using all sorts of materials to build their nests, not all of them advisable, especially human litter such as polystyrene, string and plastic. Greater Roadrunners, *Geococcyx californianus* often include snake-skins in their nest-lining, which is a bit provocative.

Perhaps the oddest nest-material, however, is used by swiftlets from the genus *Collocalia*, a group of birds which is primarily found in Asia. These live a highly aerial existence which means that they hardly ever come to land, and they are in fact incapable of perching. This makes finding nest material difficult. Their solution? To make the nest entirely out of their own dried saliva. Just before breeding the salivary glands enlarge so that they can generate enough building material.

One of the advantages of saliva is that the simple nests can be stuck anywhere, even on sheer vertical walls, as indeed they are within caves and sometimes buildings. The very odd disadvantage is that, by some strange quirk of history, human beings discovered that the nests are edible. They make up the delicacy known as bird's-nest soup, which has been used in Chinese cookery for over 400 years. The harvesting of real nests is a lucrative enterprise, and the industry is worth over US$5 billion per year.

LEFT: Glossy Swiftlets, *Collocalia esculenta*, at their nests in Malaysia.

CLEVEREST NEST-MATERIAL COLLECTION

Nest-building can be hard work. Imagine the drudgery of flying to the right place to pick up the materials, then laboriously carrying them back to the nest, where they have to be carefully arranged, and then repeating the process over and over again. Some birds will make hundreds, or even thousands of visits between the nest and the source of the nesting materials.

One bird determined to make the whole task easier is the Rosy-faced Lovebird, *Agapornis roseicollis*, of the western regions of southern Africa. It uses materials such as leaves, grass and bark for its nest, but rather than carrying them in its bill, as most birds do, it instead lodges them in the feathers of the lower back and rump. These feathers are specially adapted for carrying material, having small hooks on them to keep it in place. The bird flies back without the aerodynamic burden of holding them crosswise in the bill.

Strangely, even though there are several other species of closely related lovebirds, none of the others use this 'Look, no hands!' method.

FASTEST-FLYING BIRD

The fastest-moving bird is undoubtedly the Peregrine Falcon, *Falco peregrinus*. One of its hunting methods is to dive from height onto its prey, which is often a bird about the size of a pigeon or duck, in a manoeuvre known as a 'stoop'. The Peregrine does not usually plummet directly down, but at an angle that varies anywhere between 60° to the horizontal and less than 20°. The dive varies in distance, and sometimes it might just cover 100m (330ft), but occasionally the bird falls more than 1,000m (3,300ft), and in such cases it can attain astonishing, death-defying speeds. The hunter will take a few flaps, close its wings and let gravity accelerate it to 360km/h (223mph), a truly amazing measure for self-powered flight, and much the fastest in the animal world.

The hunter rarely actually stoops directly on to the victim – if it does so it might well kill it outright by breaking the neck or wings – but instead slows down behind the prey and swoops towards it to make a grab with the talons. Often the bird being chased is unbalanced and brought to the ground.

The Peregrine's performance in level flight is impressive – it can reach at least 110kmh (68mph) – but this isn't much different to several other bird species. Albatrosses (family Diomedeidae), Common Swifts, *Apus apus*, and even hummingbirds (family Trochilidae) can reach comparable speeds.

••

REPTILES

WORLD'S MOST DEADLY SNAKE

There is much debate about this record. The trouble is that you can measure, and express the degree of danger, in different ways; for example, the snake with the most deadly venom might not have the fierce disposition to use it. On the other hand, an aggressive and abundant snake which kills large numbers of people each year, such as the Indian Cobra, *Naja naja* (both images), of Asia, might not have quite such potent venom. If you are bitten, you probably won't care for long whether it was a Puff Adder, *Bitis arietans*, or a Black Mamba, *Dendroaspis polylepis*, that got you.

About 50,000 people die from snakebite each year in India alone, and most deaths can be attributed to a group known as the 'Big Four': the Indian Cobra (15,000 deaths per year); Common Krait, *Bungarus caeruleus* (10,000); Russell's Viper, *Daboia russelii* (25,000); and Saw-scaled Viper, *Echis carinatus* (5,000).

The snake with the most toxic venom, however, is the Inland Taipan, *Oxyuranus microlepidotus*, from Australia. A single bite from this snake contains enough venom to kill 100 people, and it only takes 30–45 minutes for the venom to act.

The snake that you would probably least prefer to meet, however, is the extremely dangerous Black Mamba of sub-Saharan Africa. This is a large and aggressive snake with a lethal bite and it is prone to attack without provocation. It is also common, and considered to be the world's fastest-moving land snake, capable of travelling at speeds of up to 20km/h (12mph). If it bites you, you might not make it, even with the best medical treatment.

OPPOSITE: Russell's Viper, *Daboia russelii*
ABOVE TOP: Inland Taipan, *Oxyuranus microlepidotus*
ABOVE BOTTOM: Saw-scaled Viper, *Echis carinatus*

LARGEST LIVING REPTILE

All the largest living reptiles are crocodiles, the largest of which is the fearsome Saltwater Crocodile, *Crocodylus porosus* (above), which is the main reason to avoid swimming in Australian billabongs. This monster, which also occurs in southern Asia, can grow to 6.3m (20.7ft) long. As with all impressive animals, plenty of other records have been claimed, some well in excess of 7m (23ft), but very large crocodiles tend to take exception to being caught and measured, so the business is fraught with difficulties.

The average length of an adult Saltwater Crocodile is actually only 4.5m (14.8ft), so well below these measurements. But that isn't much consolation if you fall into the water with one.

BIGGEST DINOSAUR BATTLE

Dinosaurs have a habit of being cantankerous with each other in the movies, often picking fights just as a human cast-member has been cornered and is there for the taking. Some of the cinema contests have been between animals that, in reality, never crossed paths and missed each other by many millions of years.

However, some titanic battles undoubtedly took place, and there is convincing evidence that some of the world's most famous animals did indeed fight to the death during the late Cretaceous period up to 65 million years ago.

In one corner is everybody's favourite baddie, *Tyrannosaurus rex*, which was undoubtedly one of the largest predatory dinosaurs ever known. It's the poster boy in a group known as therapods, the ones with huge heads packed with teeth, and with very small forelimbs. The largest complete *Tyrannosaurus* skeleton is 12.3m (40ft) long. It was probably faster-moving and far more deadly than it is usually depicted in films, being one of the most terrifying predators of all time.

In the other corner is the equally iconic dinosaur, *Triceratops horridus*, with its famous three-horned face, one above the nose and two above the eyes. Weighing in at 6–12 tonnes, 9m (30ft) long and up to 3m (10ft) tall, herbivorous *Triceratops* was either a daunting adversary or a very large hunk of flesh, depending on your individual tyrannosaur's opinion. The two undoubtedly overlapped in time, distribution and probably habitat. And so long as you accept that *Tyrannosaurus* was predatory (some suggest that it was only a scavenger), then it seems certain that this titanic struggle did indeed take place. Oh for a ringside seat!

LARGEST EXTINCT REPTILE

At present it can feel as though there is a new 'biggest dinosaur' record claimed almost every week, but that shouldn't distract us from the sheer wonder of just how enormous and mighty many of these reptiles were. The herds of enormous house-sized animals that you see in the movies truly existed, and it is sad that we missed out on seeing them by a mere 65 million years.

The largest recorded dinosaurs have all been sauropods, the giant long-necked and long-tailed dinosaurs including such well-known brands as *Brachiosaurus* and *Diplodocus*. The largest complete and mounted skeleton is of a 25m (82ft) long *Diplodocus*, but the biggest sauropods appear to be from a group from the southern continents known as the titanosaurs. The well-known *Argentinosaurus* and *Supersaurus* were perhaps over 30m (98.5ft) in length, but their remains are not complete enough to be sure. However, a new species announced during 2014 may well trump them all. It is estimated to have been an incredible 40m (131ft) in length.

....

TOP LEFT: *Tyrannosaurus* almost certainly does deserve its fearsome reputation. It might well have been the largest flesh-eating predator of all time. Imagine its prey being twice the size of a rhinoceros, and you get the idea of how large it was.

TOP RIGHT: A new claim for 'world's largest dinosaur' crops up at regular intervals, but all the largest would have been long-necked Sauropods like these *Brachiosaurus*.

STRONGEST BITE

The title of world's strongest bite alternates between two of the world's most feared predators, the Saltwater Crocodile, *Crocodylus porosus* (above), and the Great White Shark, *Carcharodon carcharius*. For the moment, the official record holder is the croc, because that is the one that has been most accurately measured.

In a study that was essentially a cross between science and a bunch of guys having a great deal of fun, a team from Florida State University used a padded device that they placed into the jaws of various living crocodiles and alligators to measure the bite force. The winner was the Saltie, with a force of 16,460 newtons (3,700 pounds per square inch, or psi). The human equivalent is a pretty pathetic 890N (200psi), while Lions, *Panthera leo*, and Spotted Hyaenas, *Crocuta crocuta*, at least generate 4,450N (1,000psi).

So what of the Great White Shark? The problem is that is has only been measured by computer and not directly.

Nonetheless, the bite force for a 6.5m (21ft) shark has been estimated at 17,790N (4,000 psi), which would outperform the crocodile. Of course, you don't actually want to be chomped by either.

As is often the case, we can at least breathe a sigh of relief that the age of the mega-chompers has passed. Back in prehistory, much bigger crocodilians and sharks existed, as well as terrifying creatures such as *T. rex*. The bite of *Tyrannosaurus* has been estimated at 57,000N (12,814psi), while there is a fossil crocodile called *Deinosuchus* that could have had a bite force of 102,750N (23,100psi) according to the computer models. The equivalent monster shark, known as *Carcharodon megalodon* (right and tooth, top right), was 16m (50ft) long and weighed 30 times as much as a Great White. Its bite may have been ten times as strong as the extant species, enough to crush a small car. It is believed that it used to chase whales and bite off their tails and flippers.

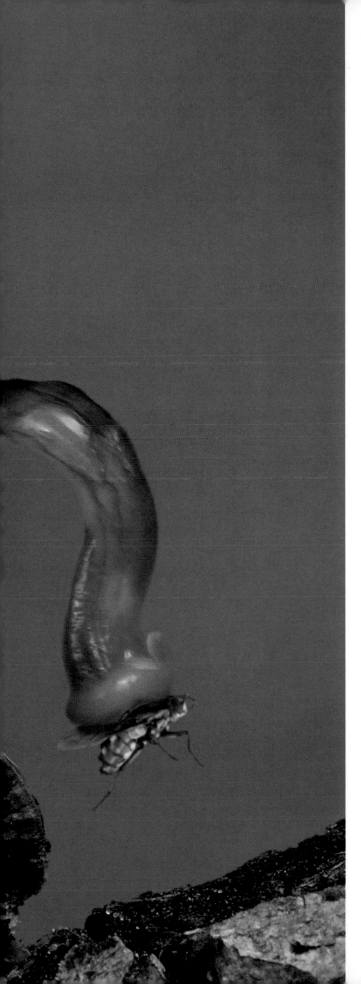

LONGEST TONGUE

The longest tongue in the animal kingdom - measuring 6m (20ft) - belongs to the Blue Whale, but this giant of the seas holds many size records. A more interesting and relevant measurement is that of the longest tongue relative to body size, in which case the winners are in the chameleon family (Chamaeleonidae) of Africa (especially Madagascar) and Eurasia. These lizards can shoot their tongues out to approximately twice their body length in some species.

The chameleon's tongue is its hunting tool of choice. While the animal itself concentrates on concealment, both by tuning its colour to the surroundings and moving very slowly, it uses its eyes, which can move independently of each other, to focus efficiently on prey. Once food is within range, the tongue shoots out towards it, sometimes connecting within 0.07 seconds. At rest the tongue coils around the tongue skeleton; at release there is something of a slingshot mechanism, which sends the tongue shooting out like a wet bar of soap being squeezed. It accelerates at a maximum of 41g-force.

Another remarkable feature is that when the tongue strikes its target it doesn't simply knock the intended prey out of range, but instead adheres powerfully to it. This results from two mechanisms; firstly, the tongue is laden with copious amounts of sticky saliva; and secondly, a lightning muscle contraction makes the surface of the tongue slightly concave, similar to the suction cup on toy arrows. In this way a chameleon can hold a prey item weighing 15 per cent of its own body weight at the end of its tongue, and then pull it in.

And what that means is that even if a chameleon didn't have the longest tongue in the animal kingdom, it certainly has the most remarkable.

Veiled Chameleon, *Chamaeleo calyptratus.*

FASTEST LIZARD

The fastest-running lizard in the world is the Black Spiny-tailed Iguana, *Ctenosaura similis*. When escaping it can attain a top speed of 34.9km/h (21.7mph), which is faster than most people can run. That is probably just as well, because in parts of Central America it is considered a delicacy, and is even farmed (along with the somewhat slower Green Iguana, *Iguana iguana*), as well as being a target for the pet trade.

TOP: Iguanas are the fastest-running living reptiles, although all the living species would have been easily outpaced by dinosaurs. Nevertheless, at top speed they could outrun most people.
OPPOSITE: It isn't easy to measure the length of the world's longest snake, since a large Reticulated Python is rarely co-operative!

LONGEST SNAKE

The question of which is the world's longest snake is one of those where a host of wild and wide-eyed claims muddy the waters. In terms of indisputable measurement, the world's longest snake is the Reticulated Python, *Python reticulatus*, which occurs in South-East Asia. One specimen of 6.95m (22.8ft) has been authenticated and a handful of specimens over 6m (19.7ft) are known.

The much better-known Green Anaconda, *Eunectes murinus*, is not the longest snake in the world, but it is the heaviest at 150kg (330lb). It might stretch to 6m or so. It is undoubtedly the most unreliably measured snake in the world; claims of anything up to 45m (148ft) stretch credulity to the limit. There has been a large reward waiting for somebody to find a confirmed specimen of 9m (30ft) or more since the early 20th century. It currently stands at US$50,000 and is yet to be claimed.

LONELIEST ANIMAL

The 'loneliest' animal in the world was, until recently, a male Galápagos Giant Tortoise, *Chelonoidis nigra* (above), of the Pinta Island subspecies *abingdonii*. This individual, known affectionately as 'Lonesome George,' died on 24 June 2012 as the very last of its kind. He was just over 100 years old. Although there are still other subspecies of Galápagos Giant Tortoises on different islands of the archipelago, the 60 sq km (23 sq mile) island of Pinta was rendered unsuitable for tortoises owing to the fact that introduced goats ran amok and destroyed much of the vegetation available to the reptiles. For at least 40 years Lonesome George represented the only Pinta Giant Tortoise in existence, and he was kept as a pet at a research station on Santa Cruz. Unfortunately he never managed to produce viable eggs with any of the females penned with him.

A poignant subscript to the story is that goats have subsequently been eliminated from Pinta.

Every time an animal becomes extinct there will be a last individual. Somewhere out there, today, there will be a comparable state of affairs, although humankind might not be aware of exactly what.

MOST REMARKABLE DEFENCE

Lizards are preyed upon by a lot of different animals, so it is not surprising that they have developed a wide range of defensive mechanisms – not least the well-known ability to shed their tail if it's in the teeth of a predator. Perhaps the oddest move – and definitely the most unnerving – is performed by a group of spiny species called horned lizards, genus *Phrynosoma* (above). When harassed by a predator they shoot out a jet of blood from the corner of the eyes, something so bizarre that you couldn't make it up. The blood surprises the attacker and also has a foul smell.

Apparently the jet is generated by the reptile shutting off the blood supply leaving the head. This builds up pressure, which is relieved by small blood vessels around the eye rupturing. The jet can shoot for more than 1m (3.2ft). You would imagine that it is very much a last resort for the lizards, and it certainly gives a new meaning to the term 'blood-shot eyes'.

AMPHIBIANS

BIGGEST FROG OR TOAD

The world's largest frog is, appropriately enough, the Goliath Frog, *Conraua goliath* (above), which is found in Africa, in Cameroon and Equatorial Guinea. It can measure 33cm (13in) from snout to vent, not including the legs, and can weigh about 3kg (6.6lb), so you couldn't easily hold it in your hand as you generally can with most other frogs. The Goliath Frog lives along fast-flowing rivers and torrents. The tadpoles appear to rely on a single plant species, *Dicraea warmingii*, for their diet. Adult frogs, meanwhile, have a broad diet of insects, other frogs and small snakes – the latter a small measure of revenge over the dozens of snakes that eat frogs.

This remarkable animal is considered a delicacy for many people in the areas where it occurs, and no doubt an adult makes a pretty hefty meal.

The biggest frog is larger than all the biggest toads of the world. The largest toad is possibly Rococo's Toad, *Rhinella schneideri*, of South America, which can grow to 25cm (10in) in length (pages 102–103).

HARDIEST FROG

Everybody knows that amphibians are cold-blooded, and the vast majority live in warm regions where intense cold isn't an issue. In temperate regions, frogs become torpid in the winter, allowing the body temperature and metabolic rate to fall and sending the animal into a hibernation-like deep sleep.

Some frogs, however, live in regions that are subject to serious cold in the winter, not least the Wood Frog, *Lithobates sylvaticus* (right), which reaches far into Alaska, USA, where the winter temperature may drop to -18°C (0°F) and rarely rises much above -9°C (16°F). In such conditions, one might expect body tissues to freeze. And that's exactly what does happen. Wood Frogs freeze in the winter, sometimes for months on end. Up to 60 per cent of their tissues become rock solid, yet in the springtime they thaw again and come back to life. It is known that a number of insects do this, but the Wood Frog is highly unusual as a vertebrate for conjuring such a rebirth. The key appears to be events which happen in the autumn, when wild Wood Frogs are subjected to regular freezing and thawing. This apparently builds up glucose in the tissues, which acts as an antifreeze in the depths of the bleak Arctic winter.

ABOVE: Golfodulcean Poison Dart Frog, *Phyllobates vittatus*.

MOST POISONOUS FROG

The world's most poisonous frog is a truly remarkable creature called the Golden Poison Dart Frog, *Phyllobates terribilis* (left), which is also the most poisonous animal known anywhere in the world. Each individual frog contains enough of a chemical, batrachotoxin, to kill 20,000 mice, or at least five or six average human beings. Bearing in mind that most frogs only harbour about 1mg of this poison, you can get an idea of its extraordinary potency.

The frogs themselves only use the poison as a defence, but famously, the Choco Emberá people of the Colombian rainforest appropriate it for their poison darts, which they use in hunting. In fact, they use the toxins of three species of frog. To obtain them from *Phyllobates aurotaenia* and *P. bicolor* they skewer the frogs on sticks and hold them over a fire until their skin exudes enough liquid for 20–30 dart tips. However, the Golden Poison Dart Frogs are different. All the hunters need to do is to hold down a living frog with sticks and rub the arrows over its skin so that the toxin saturates the tip. Once treated, the darts may then be useful for as long as two years.

ODDEST PLACE TO NURTURE THE YOUNG

You might say that frogs and toads have cornered the market in peculiar ways to look after their young. Take toads in the genus *Pipa* (above and right), which are totally aquatic species from South America. In this case the male toads press up to 100 eggs onto the female's back (two or three at a time in a laborious process). Within the next 24 hours a pad of spongy tissue swells around the eggs, almost completely encasing each one. After a time tadpoles, or even fully formed toadlets, depending on the species, hatch out of the mother's back – an arresting sight and not one for the squeamish.

Another strange strategy is practised by Darwin's Frog, *Rhinoderma darwinii*, from streams in Patagonia. The female lays eggs on damp ground and the male fertilises them with his sperm – so far so normal. Once this occurs, though, he swallows the eggs and transfers them to his vocal sac, where they are nourished for 52 days on their own yolk and some secretions from the male's skin. The male, not surprisingly, keeps quiet during this time. A fairly similar strategy is seen in the Australian Pouched Frog, *Assa darlingtoni*, except that the male waits for the eggs to hatch. He then allows the tadpoles to enter into two small pockets on his hips, where they continue their development.

But the oddest breeding strategy has to be the bizarre nurturing by the gastric brooding frogs, *Rheobatrachus* spp., of Australia. In this case the female looks after the eggs and young. She swallows the eggs but, instead of keeping them in the relatively neutral conditions of the vocal sac, she really does swallow them and they sink down into her stomach. Fortunately for them, the flow of gastric juices that normally digests the frog's food is switched off, and for 40 days or so the mother fasts as the young develop. They are eventually spat out fully formed.

This extraordinary strategy shows just how far frogs will sometimes have to go to protect their desperately vulnerable young. Tragically, the two species of gastric brooding frog, which were always rare, are now thought to be extinct.

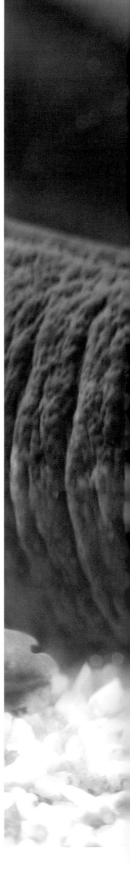

LONGEST TIME AS A JUVENILE

Quite a number of animals take many years to become adult – think of elephants, whales, tortoises, humans, and so on. However, there is a small group of animals that typically spend their whole lives in juvenile form; they mature as larvae and fail to metamorphose into adults. This is a phenomenon known as neoteny.

The most famous animal to exhibit neoteny is the Axolotl or 'Mexican Walking Fish,' *Ambystoma mexicanum* (two colour forms above and right), which is commonly kept as a pet. This amphibian exhibits an aquatic larval form similar to many of its relatives, the salamanders, with external, feather-like gills and fins for swimming. However, most salamanders eventually mature into a terrestrial, slightly lizard-like form, with rougher skin, protruding eyes and four legs. Axolotls remain in their larval state and actually breed without ever becoming terrestrial. Very occasionally, however, they do metamorphose into something very like their near-relative the Tiger Salamander, *A. tigrinum*.

Neoteny isn't the only bizarre quirk of Axolotls. They also have the capacity to regenerate limbs if these get accidentally severed, without the use of scar tissue. They can even regenerate some parts of their brain, while brain tissue and eyes, for example, can easily be transplanted from one individual to another and work perfectly well. This strange superhero-like ability is being studied closely to see whether it can be of use in medical science.

SMALLEST FROG OR TOAD

The identity of the world's smallest frog – and perhaps the world's smallest vertebrate – took a big (or small) leap forward in 2012 when researchers checked the leaf-litter on a forest floor in Papua New Guinea and found *Paedophryne amanuensis*. This midget is only 7mm (0.276in) long, although its calls are clearly audible even amidst the night-time chorus. Only slightly larger was another discovery, *Paedophryne swiftorum*. Previously, the record had been held by the Brazilian Gold Frog, *Brachycephalus didactylus*, itself 8.6–10.4mm (0.339–0.409in) long.

Watch this space, though, because now scientists know where to find them, the New Guinea leaf litter could be full of new species of tiny frogs awaiting discovery.

FISH

A Whale Shark easily dwarfs the human diver next to it. Happily these giants of the sea are harmless to people, subsisting on very small organisms.

WORLD'S LARGEST FISH

The world's largest fish is the Whale Shark, *Rhincodon typus*, named for its enormous size, which rivals that of many whales. The largest known confirmed specimen was 12.65m (41.5ft) in length and had an estimated weight of 21.5 tonnes, although as ever with these things, many larger specimens have been claimed.

The world's second largest fish, the Basking Shark, *Cetorhinus maximus*, is not too far behind; the largest specimen ever recovered was 12.27m (40.3ft). However, the average length is 6–8m (20–26ft), whereas Whale Sharks average considerably more at 9.7m (32ft).

Fortunately for the rest of the animals in the sea, both these monsters are basically filter-feeders, eating vast quantities of plankton and algae, plus occasional small fish. The Great White Shark, *Carcharodon carcharius*, the largest predatory fish, can reach about 6m (20ft) in length.

MOST UNUSUAL ESCAPE TECHNIQUE

Hagfish (class Myxini) are strange, primitive fish that look like eels but lack a vertebral column. They feed on live worms and a variety of other sea creatures, but also on dead and dying material. Imagine a giant leech with two rows of comb-like teeth and you have the idea.

Hagfish are famous (moderately) for their ability to exude large amounts of sticky mucus from their loose-fitting skin, mucus that is surprisingly useful in several situations. For one thing, hagfish can kill small prey by cluttering their bodies, including their gills, with this substance and suffocating them. And secondly, they use mucus as a defence mechanism, not unreasonably releasing their goo over the gills of any predator with the temerity to grab them in their jaws.

Another escape response of hagfish is particularly unusual. If a persistent attacker continues to keep its jaws clamped, the hagfish will simply tie its body into a travelling knot, which works its way from the head to the tail and simply levers the predator away. The hagfish can then slip away to find a hiding place.

Hagfish also use this knotting method to wipe their own slime off their bodies, and if they are trying to pull flesh off a dead body, they will sometimes tie themselves around an anchor to act as a brace while they pull. Hagfish might be weird and primitive, but that is pretty smart.

Meanwhile, the hagfish slime has some remarkable properties of strength and endurance, and scientists are looking into whether it could act as a renewable replacement for nylon or lycra. Yes, seriously.

SMALLEST FISH

There are many very small species of fish that would prove a huge disappointment to an angler. The smallest is probably the obscure *Paedocypris progenetica* which lives in Sumatra, Indonesia, and only measures 7.9–10.3mm (0.31–0.41in) long.

Fish throw up any number of curiosities. How about *Photocorynus spiniceps*, for example? In this species of anglerfish the males are only 6.0mm (0.24in) long, much smaller than *Paedocypris*, but the males spend their lives fused to the females, which are 50mm (2in) long and weigh in at about half a million times heavier than their mates. The males aren't free-swimming, so perhaps don't qualify as a separate organism.

DEEPEST-DIVING FISH

The world's deepest-diving fish is the Hadal Snailfish, *Pseudoliparis amblystomopsis*, which has been filmed at a depth of 7,700m (25,272ft, nearly 5 miles) in the Japan Trench in the western Pacific. At this depth there is absolutely no light (the fish have no eyes), it is extremely cold and the water pressure is immense – equivalent to '1,600 elephants standing on the roof of a car.' The fish survive by feeding on the dead bodies of fish and other organisms that sink to the ocean floor.

WORLD'S UGLIEST ANIMAL

Australia's Blobfish, *Psychrolutes marcidus*, is officially the world's most ugly animal. It was nominated to be the global mascot of the Ugly Animal Preservation Society when it won a poll of 11 nominations from around the animal world, with each championed by a different comedian and circulated online in 2012 and 2013.

The Ugly Animal Preservation Society has a serious purpose, which is to draw attention to the fact that disproportionate amounts of money are diverted to the conservation of attractive species such as the Giant Panda, *Ailuropoda melanoleuca*, while the less charismatic and beautiful ones are neglected, despite often being fascinating and equally deserving of protection. Whether voting for the ugliest animal achieves that purpose is open to question.

Moreover, representatives of the Blobfish (if there were any) could protest that the decision to vote for their candidate was based on photographs that were not taken in the most flattering environments. The fish, after all, lives in the deep sea, while the submitted photos are of landed specimens. When out of water, the Blobfish's abdomen flops around like jelly and the head is bloated so that the eyes are partially covered with skin, so that the impression is decidedly grotesque. By the same token, human beings may object to being photographed while unexpectedly submerged, or even when they have only just woken up in the morning.

That said, the Blobfish, even at its very best, is no beauty.

Other mascots of the Ugly Animal Preservation Society include: Humphead Wrasse, *Cheilinus undulatus* (right); Naked Mole-Rat, *Heterocephalus glaber* (see page 29); and Proboscis Monkey, *Nasalis larvatus* (below).

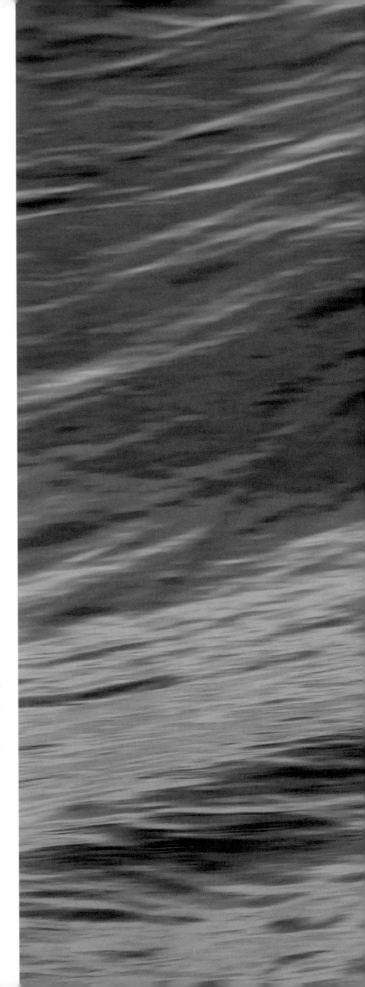

LONGEST FLIGHT BY A FISH

The flying fish (family Exocoetidae) are one of the wonders of the sea. Living all around the world, but most abundant in tropical waters, they have evolved the highly effective escape mechanism, when chased by large swimming predators, of taking to the air and gliding low over the surface of the water. This isn't a question of a quick jump out of the water and a short glide; they have been regularly reported gliding for 15 seconds non-stop, and recently a camera crew filmed an individual gliding for 45 seconds, albeit with the occasional touch of the water's surface. If this animal was travelling at the usual average gliding speed of a flying fish of 56km/h (35mph), then it would have covered 700m (2,300ft), which is probably about as far as a gliding fish could manage.

Flying fish are between 10–30cm (4–12in) in length and there are about 60 species worldwide. They all have enlarged pectoral fins, which they hold rigidly out at right angles to the body. A few species also have enlarged anal fins that provide a second pair of aerofoils to help maintain flight and control. The tail is equally important; very quick sideways movements of the tail allow the flying fish to build up maximum speed before lifting above the surface. If the speed is not sufficient, the fish can vibrate the tail at 50 beats per second until the animal is airborne.

Although flying fish usually glide just above the surface of the water, they have been recorded landing on the decks of large vessels 10m (33ft) or more above the water.

Fish don't actually fly, but they can glide for considerable distances. It is a very efficient escape response to danger in the water.

Just looking at an archer fish, you'd have no idea of its remarkable skills.

SHARPEST-SHOOTING FISH

The actress Jennifer Lawrence might appear to be handy with a bow and arrow in *The Hunger Games*, but not even she can compete for sheer consistent accuracy with the archer fish (family Toxotidae) of South-East Asia and Australasia. These remarkable freshwater fish hunt by shooting a jet of water from their mouths towards invertebrates perched above them on waterside vegetation, and they hardly ever miss. The water hits the invertebrate and dislodges it, making it easy prey as it falls to the surface. This fish will also leap up and grab prey in its jaws. It thus feeds on terrestrial invertebrates despite being aquatic itself.

The archer fish usually aims at a target at a maximum of 2m (6.5ft) above the surface of the water. It can shoot as high as 5m (16.5ft), but isn't so accurate, whereas it almost invariably hits a closer target. Young fish are not as accurate as adults, and there is evidence that they school together and learn from their peers.

Archer fish have a small groove on the roof of the mouth, and they make this an effective tube by using the tongue. The jet is produced by a powerful contraction of the gill covers, and the tube concentrates the jet. It isn't a simple process, because the shooter must compensate for refraction between air and water, one of the reasons why young fish have to practise.

Motionless in wait for prey, Anglerfishes often have cryptic colouration to disguise their appearance.

MOST EFFICIENT FISHING FISH

It wasn't humankind that first came up with the idea of a lure at the end of a rod to tempt a hungry fish – it was the fish themselves. A whole group, known as the anglerfish (order Lophiiformes), have the first few bones of their dorsal fin modified into a long, stringy filament known as the illicium, which protrudes from the forehead just above the eyes. This is fleshy and movable, and may have either a fringed or a bulbous tip, with different designs for different species. Many species can waggle the illicium about to mimic the movements of a small animal and thus attract the attention of pint-sized predators, which in turn are snatched by the anglerfish. Presumably the prey is always gobbled up before it does any damage to the lure.

Some anglerfish living in the deep sea, at depths down to 2,000m (6,560ft), have bioluminescent bacteria at the tip of the illicium, which make the lure glow in the dark. In a habitat where food is often at low density, this is a clever way to tempt small fish and crustaceans to their death.

STRANGEST SOCIETY

If you sometimes feel compelled to bemoan the society you live in, then just feel grateful that you weren't born as an Orange Clownfish, *Amphiprion percula* (right), an inhabitant of the Great Barrier Reef. There are few odder social arrangements in the animal kingdom.

Orange Clownfish live most of their lives among the tentacles of sea anemones, in this case two species called *Heteractis magnifica* and *Stichodactyla gigantea*. The fish themselves secrete a mucus that prevents the anemones discharging their poisonous nematocysts, and they also have immunity to the toxins. It is a symbiotic relationship, in which the clownfish lure other edible fish towards the anemone and also help to oxygenate the water, while the anemone provides shelter and protection.

However, within the tentacles of each anemone, space is limited to a maximum of six fish. It is advantageous for the individuals to reside within such an arrangement, because any Orange Clownfish that decided to go its own way and leave the anemone would quickly be eaten. However, the social order within the group is stifling and hierarchical. Of the six, only two breed: the largest individual – the female – and the largest male. The rest, all males, make up numbers and don't breed, and within this grouping the hierarchy continues downwards. Each fish down the pecking order is only a maximum of 80 per cent the size of the one above it. If a fish dies or departs, everybody is promoted and grows slightly bigger, while a juvenile slots in at the bottom of the hierarchy. This inflexible system may persist for many years.

Perhaps the oddest turn of events happens when the female dies, however. Remember, all the rest of the gang are males, so where do they find a new breeding female? The answer is simple: the highest-ranking male simply changes sex. The second-highest ranking male now becomes promoted to the breeding male, and proceeds to mate with the individual which was previously its male rival.

Why do the subordinate males consent to years of non-breeding activity? It would seem that they are simply waiting their turn to get to the head of the queue, first as a male and then as a female. Strange!

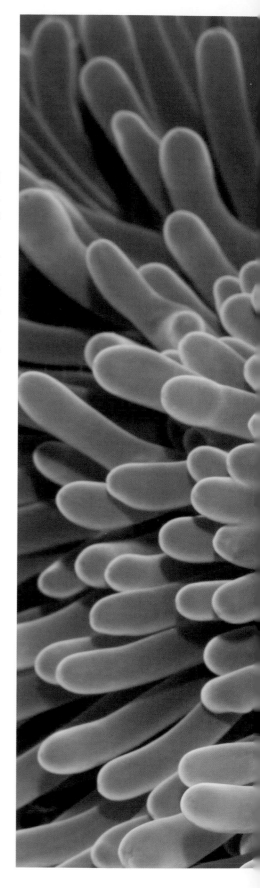

INSECTS

FASTEST-RUNNING INSECT

For a group of creatures best known for its flying ability, it is interesting to know that certain insects can also move on land pretty fast when they need to. The fastest-running insect so far measured has proven to be no less than the American Cockroach, *Periplaneta americana* (right). It can run a distance equivalent to 50 times its own body length every second, which adds up to a highly impressive 5.4km/h (3.4mph), or about the walking speed of an average human.

Having said that, if cockroaches were the size of humans, and their ratio of speed to body length remained the same, they would be able to walk at 330km/h (205mph). They do have six legs, though.

INSECTS: FASTEST WING-BEAT

If you've ever tried to flap your hands as fast as possible in order to simulate flying, you'll realise how pathetically bad we humans are at this. So you might be especially awestruck to realise that certain species of small flies, including midges and mosquitoes, can flap their wings at a rate of more than 1,000 times per *second*. This is what produces the whining sound in flight. The actual record is held by a midge in the genus *Forcipomyia*, with a rate of 1,046 beats per second, but this is quite likely to be broken as soon as somebody decides to measure a few more species.

How could any animal possibly beat its wings so fast? Well, perhaps the question should be asked – why not? Our arm-flapping rate and even that of some larger insects, is restricted by the speed of transmission of nerve impulses that cause muscles to contract. However, in the case of very small flies, the action of muscles and nerves is not in synchrony, and the flapping depends on a cyclical deformation of the animal's thorax.

LEFT: Midges and mosquitos may not be everybody's favourites, but the fact that they can flap their wings 1,000 times a second is still impressive.

LARGEST DRAGONFLY

The world's largest dragonfly isn't technically a dragonfly at all, but actually a damselfly. Damselflies (suborder Zygoptera) are the very elegant forms of dragonfly which usually rest their wings behind their back, or slightly open at rest. True dragonflies (suborder Anisoptera) hold their wings out horizontally at rest. Anyhow, the daddy of them all is known as *Megaloprepus caerulatus* and occurs in Costa Rica. Its body measures up to 12cm (4.7in) long and its wingspan has been measured at 19.1cm (7.5in).

Of course, as so often with animals, this size is completely dwarfed by many fossil specimens. In the Carboniferous period of 300 million years ago, well before the age of the dinosaurs, *Meganeura monyi*, had a wingspan of 75cm (29.5in).

LARGEST WASP

Wasps (known as 'yellowjackets' in North America) are well worth avoiding in most parts of the world, but the largest species of all, the Asian Giant Hornet, *Vespa mandarinia* (above), is definitely not one to mess with. This impressive creature can grow up to 5cm (2in) in length, and it has something of the temperament to match. It is highly predatory, feeding on a variety of other insects, with a particular liking for mantises. It will attack colonies of bees to raid their nests for honey, and it is said that about 50 hornets can wipe out a colony of more than 50,000 bees in less than day, mainly by decapitating them with their formidable mandibles.

To go along with size, speed – they can apparently fly at 40km/h (25mph) – and aggression, Asian Giant Hornets also have an extremely painful sting. Humans attacked in the area where the hornets occur, from Japan and China west to India and Sri Lanka, quite often die as a result. For example, there were 42 fatalities in 2013 in just one province of China – Shaanxi.

One eminent entomologist has referred to these insects as "the wasp analogue of a pit bull" with "a face that looks like you just can't reason with it." Nice.

NOISIEST INSECT

While not the noisiest in terms of pure loudness, the animal that makes the loudest sound relative to its size is an aquatic bug found in Europe called *Micronector scholtzi*, which is a type of water boatman or 'backswimmer' (left). It is only 8.0mm (0.31in) long, but its chirps can measure as much as 108 decibels, as noisy as a building site.

Bizarrely, the bug makes its chirp by rubbing its penis against its belly, so presumably it also has the noisiest reproductive organ in the world.

MOST DANGEROUS ANIMAL TO HUMANS

We might not run away when we meet them, as we would do for a Polar Bear, *Ursus maritimus*, or a Lion, *Panthera leo*, but by far the most dangerous animals to humans are mosquitoes (family Culicidae). These small members of the typical fly order Diptera carry a number of diseases that are harmful to humans. It is estimated that 700 million people every year develop an infection carried by a mosquito, and deaths frequently approach 1 million annually.

The list of diseases spread by mosquitoes makes grim reading. The worst is malaria, which kills half a million people per year on its own, and is spread by the *Anopheles* mosquito. Another nasty character is called *Aedes aegypti*, which spreads both yellow fever – which causes 30,000 deaths per year despite the fact that there is an effective vaccine – and dengue fever – which causes 25,000 deaths per year but is usually unpleasant rather than fatal. The roll-call continues with West Nile virus, filariasis and several types of encephalitis, each of which may be spread by several types of mosquito.

It should perhaps be noted that the mosquitoes don't directly kill humans, as a large predator does by the clamping of its jaws. The actual agent of death in malaria is a protozoan of the genus *Plasmodium*, while diverse creatures such as viruses, bacteria and worms are the real baddies in the other diseases and infections. However, the mosquito is still implicated in the crime – it is the getaway driver, if nothing else. It carries the diseases between hosts, and without its work as a vector these maladies would in theory be wiped out.

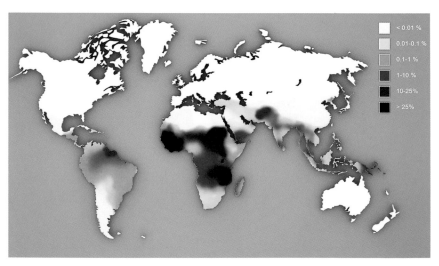

	< 0.01 %
	0.01-0.1 %
	0.1-1 %
	1-10 %
	10-25%
	> 25%

ABOVE: Malaria Areas and Risks.
RIGHT: It's a curious fact that the world's most dangerous animal is not at all frightening. Mosquitos are indirectly responsible for hundreds of thousands of human deaths every year.

HAPPIEST ENDING

We all have to die, so the most we can expect, perhaps, is to go in a state of happiness. And that's certainly the case for the males of some species of praying mantis (order Mantodea). In captive specimens, and at least sometimes in the wild, mantids demonstrate a curious phenomenon known as sexual cannibalism. That is, during the sex act, one animal (in this case the female) eats the other.

Mantids are highly predatory animals with excellent vision, and are most famous for their habit of staying still and concealed, and then making a lightning grab with their powerful forefeet when prey comes within range. The females attract a mate by sending out pheromones, but their reaction to approaching males varies according to their state of satiation. If they are especially hungry they might simply treat a hopeful male as food on first meeting, but usually a male can at least mount the female. And this is where a male's curious end might occur. If, during sex, the female begins to devour the male, the transfer of sperm will continue uninterrupted – and indeed, may be enhanced.

It is a bizarre sight indeed to see two mantids in the mating position while the female unconcernedly begins to make a meal of the male's head, chewing it unceremoniously like we might munch lettuce or a carrot. However, the males have no choice but to take the risk and, so long as they actually succeed in inseminating the female, can perish relishing a job well done.

LEAST GLAMOROUS COLONY JOB

Imagine it: you live in a colony of thousands of your own kind, like a bee, ant, termite or wasp. Presumably it is noisy, hot, smelly and busy. It is a seething mass of insect activity, quite similar to a human city but a great deal more co-operative and co-ordinated.

In every large colony there are dirty jobs, but surely the least glamorous – and one that is practised by only 1 per cent of workers – is the undertaker. This is the ant or bee that locates the dead and carries them away from the nest. It falls to middle-aged workers to do this, and undertakers are also charged with removing general debris and muck. Honey bees often carry their dead 100–200m (330–660ft) away from the hive before dropping them.

Happily, no specialised caste exists that only acts as an undertaker; it is a part-time occupation and individuals which do this will also carry out other tasks such as building the comb and storing food. But in the case of bees, the task of removal of the dead will occupy them sometimes for days on end. Among ants, once an individual has acted once as an undertaker, it won't then be allowed close to the queen or larvae, in case of infection.

MOST COLD-TOLERANT INSECT

Insects are famously indestructible, so nobody will be surprised to know that some can survive at astonishingly low temperatures, especially as larvae. What is surprising, however, is that the current record-holder is a fly from tropical West Africa. Known as *Polypedilum vanderplanki* (it was on the tip of your tongue, wasn't it?), a group of dried larvae survived after being exposed to liquid helium down to -270°C (-454°F) for 5 minutes. The larvae of this small fly are adapted to cope with extreme desiccation, which probably accounts for their remarkable temperature resistance.

The most impressive tolerance of cold by an adult insect is by a beetle that lives in the soil in Arctic regions. *Pterostichus brevicornis* can withstand temperatures down to -87°C (-125°F), because of the antifreeze properties of glycerol in its tissues. The Arctic winter must be a breeze.

OPPOSITE: The female mantis is deadlier than the male — indeed, male mantids in search of a breeding partner often end up the same way as this damselfly.

BIGGEST INSECT

Several species of insects vie with each other to be the world's largest insect. The 'winner' is usually quoted as the goliath beetle, *Goliathus goliatus*, which undoubtedly has the heaviest larva of any insect, up to 115g (4.0oz), while the adults themselves are hardly small, measuring in at 50g (1.75oz) and 10cm (4in) long. Then, in 2011, entomologists weighed a captive female of the cricket-like Little Barrier Island Giant Weta, *Deinacrida heteracantha*, and discovered that it tipped the scales at 71g (2.5oz) and was also 8.5cm (3.4in) long. Bearing in mind that this was a captive animal reared in ideal conditions, the record is a little suspect. Those championing the case of the Goliath Beetle have been complaining ever since, while their charges, one suspects, have stomped moodily off to the gym to get some more weight on.

Joking aside, there are actually five species of beetles that, at least in the wild, are normally heavier than the giant wetas. These are the goliath beetles *G. goliatus*, *G. regius*, *Megasoma elaphas*, *M. actaeon* and the unrelated *Titanus giganteus* (the names give it away somewhat).

Meanwhile, in 2012 explorers discovered the longest-bodied insect in the world, in Borneo. Predictably enough, it is a stick insect, in this case named *Phobaeticus chani*, and it is 56.7 cm (22.4in) long with legs extended, while the body alone is 35.7cm (14.1in).

LEFT: Most of the world's largest insects are beetles.

LONGEST INSECT MIGRATION

Insect migrations can be every bit as impressive as movements by birds or mammals. There is even evidence that moths, for example, can navigate using magnetic fields and day-flying insects use the sun, together with an internal clock. The distances that insects travel, whether self-powered or at the mercy of the winds, can be astonishing.

The best-known lengthy insect migration is that carried out by the Monarch butterfly, *Danaus plexippus* (above right), in North America. In autumn adults depart from the eastern side of the continent and head for groves of Oyamel trees, *Abies religiosa*, in central Mexico (above left). The journey may take them as far as 3,200km (2,000 miles) one way. However, one tagged male is known to have flown from Ontario to Mexico and back to Austin, Texas, covering at least 4,638km (2,880 miles). Interestingly, Monarchs from the west of North America winter instead in California, while some southern populations are non-migratory.

Another impressive movement has been noted for the Desert Locust, *Schistocerca gregaria* (oppsoite top). In October 1989 there was a large arrival of this African insect in the West Indies and northern South America. It was clear

from weather analysis that they had been carried across the Atlantic Ocean by a storm system, a total distance of 4,500km (2,800 miles) – and that's in addition to any distance travelled within Africa.

Just recently it has been discovered that a dragonfly called the Globe Skimmer, *Pantala flavescens* (opposite bottom), undertakes a migration across the Indian Ocean to trump every other known insect movement. Large numbers appear in southern India in October each year with the monsoon, and then head out southwards to the Maldives, arriving late in the month. After a short time they seem to head south, following the path of a weather system known as the Intertropical Convergence Zone. The insects fly high, at least 1,000m (3,280ft) above ground – they have been recorded as high as 6,300m (20,670ft) – and allow the winds to blow them towards the Seychelles and eventually Africa, where they breed. They then return, in several generations, using a similar path back to India to meet the next monsoon. If this migratory pathway is proven, the species has a back and forth migration of 14,000–18,000km (8,700–11,200 miles).

LARGEST BUTTERFLY

The world's largest butterfly is Queen Alexandra's Birdwing, *Ornithoptera alexandrae*, an extremely rare species found in a small corner of Oro Province in northern Papua New Guinea. Females may measure 29–31cm (11.4–12.2in) in wingspan, while males are smaller but much more colourful. The colour is a sign to potential predators that they are distasteful, and indeed the caterpillar feeds on toxic plants. Queen Alexandra's Birdwing now occurs in only seven locations and is threatened by oil-palm production and logging.

The image above shows a closely related birdwing species from Australia.

LARGEST MOTH

Leaving aside the fact that moths and butterflies are really much the same – butterflies are simply showy day-flying moths – the world's largest nocturnal moth is about the same size as the largest butterfly. The moth with the greatest wingspan is the splendidly named White Witch, *Thysania agrippina*, which has touched 30cm (12in) but is usually within the range 27–28cm (10.5–11in). It is a common and widespread species of Central and South America, sometimes straying into the United States.

The Atlas Moth, *Attacus atlas* (right), of South-East Asia is nearly as big, and it actually holds the record for the largest surface area of the wings, an impressive 400cm^2 (62in2). It also has a chunkier body than the White Witch, but not quite the wingspan, measuring 26.2cm (10.3in).

Worker termites attend to the outsize queen.

BEST INTERIOR DESIGN

Some of the best examples of building in the animal kingdom are undertaken by the smallest, most humble creatures, and the remarkable mounds built by termites ('termitaria') are a good example. Termites are cool, in every sense.

Although many species of termites live in trees or make small, insignificant mounds, the ones that make landscape-shaping towers are the best known. The towers are constructed out of soil, termite saliva and dung, and although they have hard outer walls, these are quite brittle and highly porous. The shape of the mound itself is significant; some are wedge-shaped, with their narrowest corner pointing in the direction of the hottest midday sun, to soak up the least heat.

Within large termite mounds there is a very complicated air-convection system which keeps the inner mound at a stable temperature. Just inside the outer walls is a complex labyrinth of small passageways that allows fresh air from the outside to penetrate into the mound. Below the nest is a cellar, where remarkable narrow plates absorb the heat from the colony above and condense the air around them, causing cooling. The cellar also has paths leading down to the water table, a source of cool air that is funnelled by special tubes into the main colony. All in all there is a highly sophisticated air-conditioning system that keeps the core of the colony at a constant temperature all year round. It does not vary by more than plus or minus a single degree.

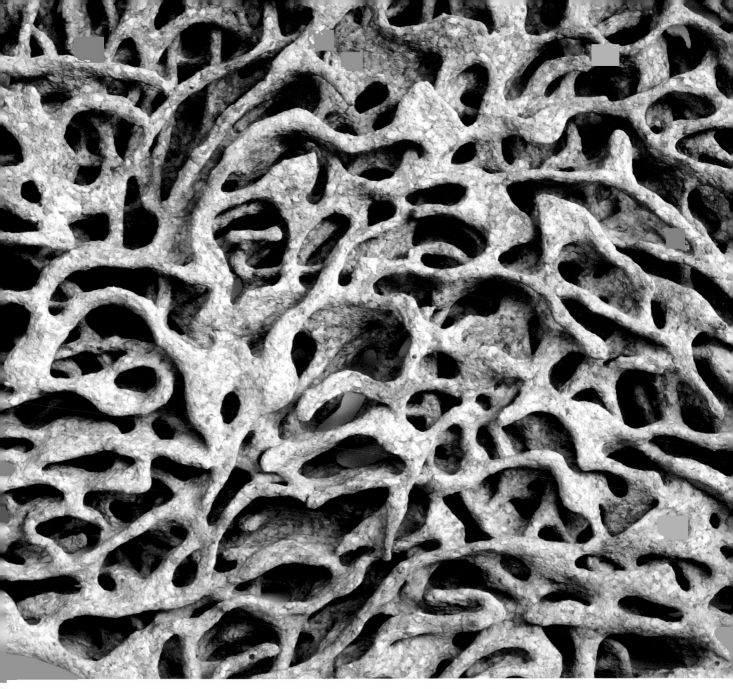

The termite mound is an astonishingly complex structure, with multiple layers and passageways.

That's not all. At or near ground-level, at the heart of the colony, is the chamber of the queen and her consort, the king. The queen may churn out thousands of eggs a day, and she lives in relative comfort in a large area reserved just for the royal family and its attendants. Other chambers are used to store food gathered by the workers outside and, remarkably, some food is actually propagated by the insects themselves. The termites chew the supplies and defecate upon them, whereupon a special fungus grows on the faeces. When they are hungry, the colony members visit these 'gardens' to eat the fungi, thereby obtaining even more nutriment from the food store.

With its air-conditioning, weather- and predator-proof outer walls, food stores and fungus gardens, the termites' nest is one of the true architectural marvels of nature.

MOST COMMITTED DEFENCE

Termites (order Isoptera) are sociable insects that live in large colonies with a communal nest, good examples being the tall earthen towers of northern Australia that dot the landscape like strange sculptures (main picture). Within the colony, different individuals have different functions; some look after the queen and king, others look for food, and so on. Another caste is charged with defence, because nests are a rich resource and can be invaded both by other termites and by ants.

The defending caste is often little more than a suicide squad. An individual soldier termite is ill-equipped to fight off many ants, but it will sacrifice itself in order to help delay an invasion, giving workers the chance to hurriedly close off tunnels into the heart of the nest. Termites will position their bodies at hole-entrances to defend them; when one falls, another immediately takes its place.

Even more remarkable, however, is a defence method that has recently been described for *Neocapritermes taracua*, a termite living in northern South America. In this case the older defenders are distinctive for having a blue mark on their abdomen. These spots are external pouches that contain a toxic potion of copper-containing proteins (hence the colour). When an ageing defender is attacked, its 'package' of toxins ruptures explosively, releasing the lethal chemicals. Most invading termites that touched the liquid were killed, along with the sacrificial defender. A prime example of chemical warfare in nature.

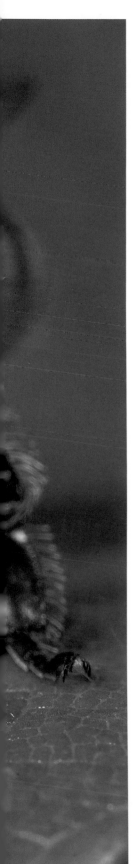

ABOVE: Parasites emerging from the still-living body of a caterpillar
LEFT: Honey Bees give directions to their peers towards nectar sources

WORST ABUSE OF A HOST

The natural world is a pretty heartless arena, with copious examples of violence and death, but very little compares to the sheer nastiness of what parasitoids sometimes do to their hosts. A good example is the parasitic wasp *Hymenoepimecis argyraphaga* of Costa Rica, an animal with despicable plans for the spider *Leucauge argyra*, which occurs in Central America north to the United States. When wasp meets spider, it stings its host, rendering it paralysed – and doomed. The wasp duly lays an egg on the spider's abdomen and, once it hatches, the larva takes advantage of its host by feasting on its internal fluids for a number of days, but never enough to kill it. It then, through means unknown, suddenly rouses the spider into action. The dead-spider-walking dismantles its own web and builds a new rudimentary one with just a few strands. Its grisly task complete, the spider is now relieved of the last of its body fluids, finally putting it out of its misery. Meanwhile, the larva spins a cocoon on the strands of the web, out of reach of predators, and completes its development in peace.

BEST INSECT CODE

As everybody knows, Honey Bees, *Apis mellifera*, live in large colonies. In the summer months the worker bees spend much of their time collecting nectar from flowers, which is brought to the colony and converted into honey. In order to facilitate the collection of nectar, returning workers laden with plant products pass on the details of their trips to other workers, by means of a code transmitted by a special display known as a 'waggle dance.'

The way in which a bee dances indicates the position of good nectar resources to other workers, communicating both the direction and distance of a rich resource. When the flowers are precisely in line with the sun, the worker dances up the vertical cone, and if the nectar-rich flowers lie at any angle left or right the bee dances at the corresponding angle to the vertical on the comb. Meanwhile, the distance of the nectar source is indicated by the duration of the waggle-run.

This is neat enough but, amazingly, if a bee is detained in the hive for some time before being able to communicate its instructions, it will adjust its dance to compensate for any movement in the sun in the meantime.

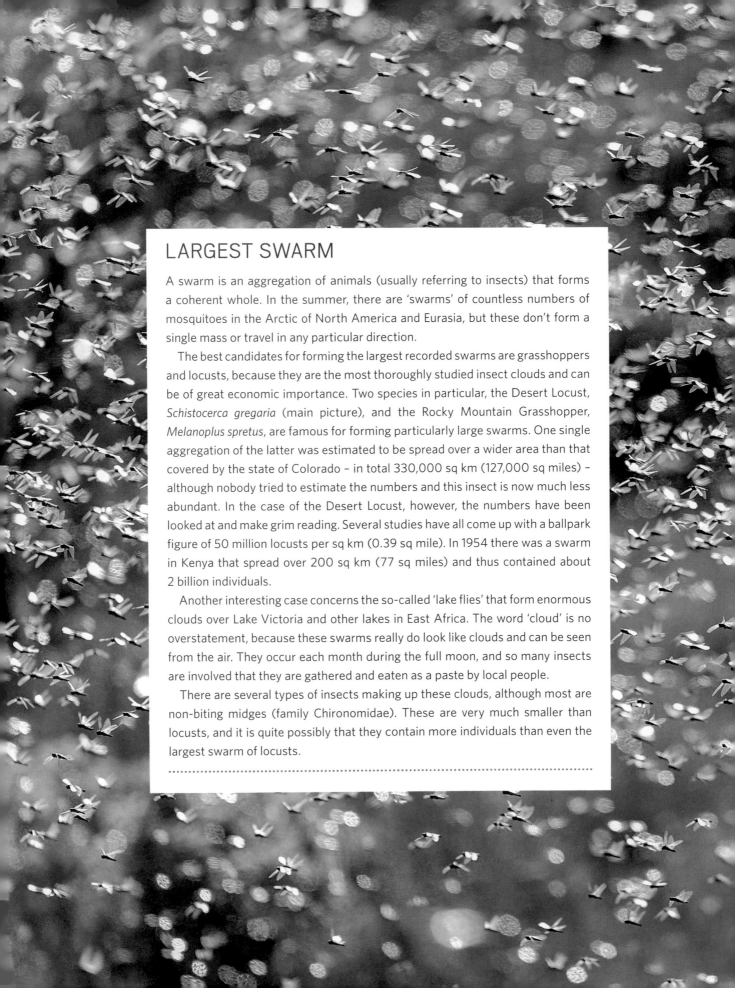

LARGEST SWARM

A swarm is an aggregation of animals (usually referring to insects) that forms a coherent whole. In the summer, there are 'swarms' of countless numbers of mosquitoes in the Arctic of North America and Eurasia, but these don't form a single mass or travel in any particular direction.

The best candidates for forming the largest recorded swarms are grasshoppers and locusts, because they are the most thoroughly studied insect clouds and can be of great economic importance. Two species in particular, the Desert Locust, *Schistocerca gregaria* (main picture), and the Rocky Mountain Grasshopper, *Melanoplus spretus*, are famous for forming particularly large swarms. One single aggregation of the latter was estimated to be spread over a wider area than that covered by the state of Colorado – in total 330,000 sq km (127,000 sq miles) – although nobody tried to estimate the numbers and this insect is now much less abundant. In the case of the Desert Locust, however, the numbers have been looked at and make grim reading. Several studies have all come up with a ballpark figure of 50 million locusts per sq km (0.39 sq mile). In 1954 there was a swarm in Kenya that spread over 200 sq km (77 sq miles) and thus contained about 2 billion individuals.

Another interesting case concerns the so-called 'lake flies' that form enormous clouds over Lake Victoria and other lakes in East Africa. The word 'cloud' is no overstatement, because these swarms really do look like clouds and can be seen from the air. They occur each month during the full moon, and so many insects are involved that they are gathered and eaten as a paste by local people.

There are several types of insects making up these clouds, although most are non-biting midges (family Chironomidae). These are very much smaller than locusts, and it is quite possibly that they contain more individuals than even the largest swarm of locusts.

SHORTEST ADULT LIFESPAN

Many familiar insects live for a surprisingly short time: many moths, butterflies, beetles and dragonflies only survive for a couple of weeks or so in the adult stage, especially in temperate regions. This, however, may be after a year or more spent as an egg, larva or pupa, meaning that the individual itself lives for much longer. However, for sheer brevity of appearance as a fully-formed adult, few if any can compete with mayflies (order Ephemeroptera). These primitive winged insects have large, lacy wings that are held together above the back when at rest, and most also have three elegant hair-like tails. They are usually seen in dancing flight over rivers and lakes.

Mayflies actually have two adult stages, both lasting for only a short time, and sometimes only for hours. The final stage, indeed, may emerge and be dead within half an hour (without taking into account those perishing from predation or misadventure), although this is unusual. However, it is an existence full of purpose. Light winds help to disperse the flying insects, and once airborne they quickly search for a mate. The 'dancing' mayflies are a mating swarm, composed of males on the lookout, and the females fly into them, quickly becoming hitched without any time to get to know their suitor. Once mated the males die very quickly. The females lay their eggs and also die within hours. No adult from either gender is physically able to feed as they lack any mouthparts, and the process of hatching, flying and mating quickly exhausts them.

MOST AGGRESSIVE GARDENERS

The Amazonian rainforest is famous worldwide for its biodiversity, and this is reflected in many aspects of nature, including trees – in one study researchers found 1,100 species of trees in an area of just 25ha (62 acres). It is therefore surprising that, here and there, small patches of forest are inhabited by just a single tree species. This is so strange that in a part of Peru where this happens the areas are thought to be inhabited by an evil forest spirit. Scientists duly call them 'devil's gardens.'

It turns out that devil's gardens are caused by ants. A recently studied example concerns an ant called *Myrmelochista schumanni*, which lives inside the stems of a forest tree called *Duroia hirsuta*. Not only do the ants protect the trees physically from grazing by herbivores (they bite), but it turns out that they also remove the trees' opposition. Remarkably, when a seedling of another tree species takes hold in the devil's garden, the ants inject poisonous formic acid directly into its leaves, thereby killing it, sometimes in as little as 24 hours.

In the largest devil's garden recorded to date, there were 328 *Duroia hirsuta* trees spread over 1,300 sq metres (14,000 sq feet). It is thought that, owing to its size, this devil's garden has been present for 800 years.

LONGEST FLY

You might read this and think: "what kind of an odd record is this?" As it happens, there is no such thing as the 'longest fly' in the world. However, if you write the name down, you will find that there is a Soldier Fly (order Diptera, subfamily Pachygastrinae) called *Parastratiosphecomyia stratiosphecomyioides*. This happens to be the longest scientific name in use in the world. The insect is from Thailand and Malaysia.

OPPOSITE: Mayflies are famous for their short lifespans, which may last just for a few hours in the adult stage. However, many live for much longer in larval form before hatching out.

LONGEST LIFECYCLE

A lifecycle is defined as the sequence of events from an individual's least developed state (an egg) to its most developed (an adult). In many animals there are several different stages, the best-known being insects, such as butterflies, that progress from egg to larva, through to pupa, and finally adult.

The length of time that these stages take in totality varies greatly between species and often between individuals of a species. It is also a very difficult aspect of life-history to study, because to be accurate in measurement you need to set your clock to zero when in possession of viable eggs.

Nonetheless, there are some interesting measurements of very long lifecycles. The record-holder might be the wood-boring beetle *Buprestis aurulenta*, with the adults finally emerging 51 years after the initial larval infestation was noted. Similarly long delays have been noted in this species and also in *Eburia quadrigeminata* (40 years from birch wood). However, later infestations could never quite be ruled out in these cases so, while the beetles are known to show considerable variation in their times of emergence, the figures cannot be proven beyond doubt.

A far more remarkable and fascinating case involves three species of cicada in North America. These are called *Magicicada septemdecim*, *M. cassini* and *M. septendecula* and, bizarrely, all complete their lifecycles in a fixed time period of 17 years. Each species occurs in a slightly different habitat, and each member of the species emerges at about the same time, so that one year in 17 there is a local 'plague' of one species or another. Huge numbers of males gather together into so-called 'chorus centres' to attract mates. They live for about six weeks and then die, while their eggs hatch into instars which live 30cm (12in) or so underground, feeding on plant juices. If an individual emerges one year early or late, it misses the mating swarms and is a lonely cicada indeed.

Some other species from the genus *Magicicada* mature at 13 years rather than 17, but all other cicadas have variable emergence or emerge every year.

RIGHT: *Magicicada* lives up to its name. The species may live in larval form for 17 years before emerging, all at once, in swarms.

MOST EFFICIENT USE OF SLAVES

It isn't only humans that use forced labour; ants do as well. Some species of ants cannot survive without slave labour, while others seem to look for slaves when the need arises. Either way, they are known as slave-making ants and the process of acquiring forced labour is coyly known as 'dulosis'. It occurs between species, with one species using another species, or set of species, as potential slaves.

The way that slave-making ants work is to launch a raid on a neighbouring nest and kidnap the pupae, rather than the adults. The pupae hatch into slavery and are put to the general work of the colony, such as rearing the broods of their captors and feeding the workers. The workers of the host species are specialised in making further raids. They may capture 14,000 pupae in a summer season.

Slave-making ants almost always raid closely-related species in nearby colonies. When word gets out that the colony needs a fresh influx of slaves, individuals make scouting visits to their neighbours' nests. If conditions are deemed to be suitable, they leave a pheromone trail and the specialised raiders follow. Normally the hosts flee, since they will usually lose if they fight, but on the occasions that they put up resistance there can be serious casualties on both sides.

Normally, the individuals brought up as slaves buy in completely to looking after the welfare of their captors, perhaps controlled by the all-pervading pheromone smell of the foreign species. So indoctrinated can they become that they even join in with raiding parties, even ones that return to their home nest. On other occasions, however, they have been known to rebel, taking revenge by killing the pupae and young of their captors.

LAND

INVERTEBRATES

FASTEST LAND SNAIL

Snails are famous for being slow, of course, not fast. Hence it is quite inevitable that, somewhere in the world, somebody would think of staging the World Snail-racing Championships (see previous spread). Not entirely surprisingly, it was dreamed up in England, a land full of eccentrics.

Thus we know that the world's fastest recorded land snail was a Garden Snail, *Helix aspersa*, called Archie that covered a 33cm (13in) course in 2 minutes in Longhan, England, in 1995. That only equates to 0.0028m/s (0.0092ft/s), but it hasn't been beaten in the subsequent 20 years, so could be considered fast.

LARGEST SPIDER'S WEB

The world's largest spider's web was discovered only in 2010, on the island of Madagascar. It is made by the Darwin's Bark Spider, *Caerostris darwini* (left), and the reason that it's so big is not because it is used to catch large prey, but because it is slung across a river. It is basically a trap attached on either side of the water, and some of the anchoring lines are up to 25 *metres* (82ft) long. The trap in the middle can be as large as 2.8 sq metres (30 sq ft) in area.

These remarkable webs are highly effective at catching insects flying over the water – up to 32 wrapped insects have been found in a single one.

The only question is – how do the spiders manage to get across the river to anchor their web on both sides? That question is yet to be answered.

HIGHEST-LIVING ANIMAL

It is perfectly possible for small flying insects or web-transported spiders to be whisked by thermals or thunderstorms up to almost unimaginable heights above the ground, but whether they survive up there or not nobody knows.

However, the animal that lives as a permanent resident at higher altitude than any other in the world, happens to be a spider. Known as the Himalayan Jumping Spider *Euophrys omnisuperstes*, this remarkable arthropod lives at altitudes of up to 6,700m (22,000ft) on Mount Everest, hiding away in rock fissures.

Now, bearing mind that spiders are predators, one might presume that this small spider's prey would be neighbours adapted to similar altitude, but this seems not to be the case. Instead, the jumping spider seems to subsist on the frozen bodies of small insects brought up by the wind.

This species' scientific name means, appropriately enough, 'standing above everything.'

LARGEST SPIDER

Movie heroines need not worry; even the world's largest spiders are small enough to be squashed by a human boot. They are physiologically unable to carry their heavy exoskeleton beyond certain limits. But the biggest spiders are still a formidable bunch and you wouldn't want to meet any of them in a dark corner (unfortunate that, because that's exactly where you might find them).

The biggest spider is generally regarded to be the Goliath Bird-eating Spider, *Therophosa blondi* (above), which is found in the coastal rainforests of northern South America. The largest specimen, collected in Venezuela in 1965, had a leg-span of 28cm (11in) – famously big enough to cover a large dinner plate – and weighed in at 50g (1.76oz). Spiders like this are big enough to catch mice and birds, but despite having fangs of up to 2cm (0.8in) long, they are harmless to humans (unless they give you a heart attack, of course).

The largest non-tarantula spider is almost certainly the Giant Huntsman, *Heteropoda maxima*, which was discovered in a cave in Laos in 2001. As every Australian knows, huntsman spiders are leggy and fast, and this is the leggiest of all, with a span of 30cm (12in). It doesn't approach a tarantula in weight, but it is still the stuff of many peoples' nightmares.

MOST DANGEROUS SPIDER

It might not be the most famous of the dangerous spiders, but the Brazilian Wandering Spider, *Phoenutria nigriventer* (above), actually carries the most toxic venom. It lives up to its name by wandering around to hunt (it is related to the Wolf Spiders) and unfortunately will sometimes serendipitously find itself among cultivated flowers or fruit, such as bananas, where it comes into contact with humans. It has to be provoked to bite, but it can and does kill. Its scientific name *Phoenutria* is the Greek word, appropriately enough, for 'murderess' and one of the side-effects of its bite in humans is extreme pain in a man's penis.

The Sydney Funnel-web, *Atrax robustus*, is only the second most dangerous spider in the world, although that is scant comfort if you've been bitten by one. A bite can cause death within 15 minutes, but there is now a highly effective anti-venom widely available in south-eastern Australia, where it occurs. This has drastically reduced the death rate for humans bitten by this species, which was the scourge of the early settlers. One of the reasons why funnel-webs are so dangerous is that they are often fearless and aggressive, and they should be treated with extreme caution.

MOST LEGS

It will surprise nobody that the creatures with the most legs are the millipedes, arthropods in the group known as the Myriapoda. Despite the name, no millipede has yet been found with 1,000 legs, but one species comes relatively close. It is a very obscure species from California called *Illacme plenipes*, and its record total was 750 legs (375 pairs). You might expect members of the same species to have similar numbers of legs but they don't, and most specimens actually have 600 (obviously a few dozen pairs of legs here and there makes little difference).

One of the most surprising things about *Illacme plenipes* is that, rather than being long and big as you might expect, it is small for a millipede, measuring less than 3cm (1.2in) in length. Those limbs are certainly packed in.

Centipedes are also myriapods and, as their name implies, they have fewer legs than millipedes, but some do have up to about 300. The odd thing about them is that they always have an uneven number of pairs – 17, 21, 35 and so on – so no centipede can have 50 pairs of legs and fit their name perfectly.

There are 12,000 species of millipedes known, but none of them have 1,000 legs. This giant millipede is from Asia.

COYEST MALE SUITOR

Male red velvet mites (subclass Acari, family Trombidiidae) look brightly coloured and, for mites, quite attractive. The males of the species, however, act as though they have a severe self-image problem. When it comes to sex, their coyness is perhaps unparalleled in the animal kingdom.

Rather than involving themselves in the sex act, red velvet mites instead discretely detach their spermatophores and place them at some tasteful location, such as the tip of a grass stem or on a twig. They then produce a silken trail that leads to the spot, and then rely completely upon a female coming across their handiwork and being impressed. A suitably won-over female will simply sit on the spermatophore and thus be fertilized.

This method of remote sex has an obvious disadvantage. If another male mite comes across the 'garden,' he will destroy it and replace the spermatophore with one of his own.

LEFT: Male Red Velvet Mites leave small packages of sperm in prominent places such as the tips of grass stems. But they discreetly avoid the opposite sex.

STRANGEST PLACE TO MATE

Slugs, land-based molluscs related to snails, are sluggish, by definition. They are best thought of as shell-less snails, although some do have a very small, useless (vestigial) shell on their back. They often repulse people and don't help their reputation by eating our treasured garden plants.

Being essentially slow but steady movers sliding on a carpet of their own slime, slugs would appear to be terrestrial down to the ground. So where do you think one of the world's largest species, the Great Grey Slug, *Limax maximus*, of Europe mates? Well, of course, it has to be – in the air!

To be fair, Great Grey Slugs don't fly. However, their mating ritual is no less astonishing for that. On a warm night in summer, two individuals come together (both are hermaphrodite) and circle and lick each other, sometimes for an hour or more. This is only the foreplay. After some time, they both begin to climb up the trunk of a tree or a wall and find their way to a horizontal edge. Here they will lower each other, entwined, on a strong cord of mucus, like a pair of rather naughty high-wire artists. On occasions the slugs will let themselves down as much as a metre or more, and once they are dangling in their air, they will extend their reproductive organs to touch and intertwine – this is the act of mating. Bizarrely, their reproductive organs are a translucent sky blue colour, which must make them obvious. Then again, by being suspended in mid-air, the slugs are presumably relatively safe from many predators.

After copulating, one slug climbs back up the acrobatic cord and slides away. Meanwhile the other partner may make its own way back, eating the mucus as it goes, or will lower itself elegantly back to the ground. After a month or so, each will lay its own set of eggs.

MARINE

INVERTEBRATES

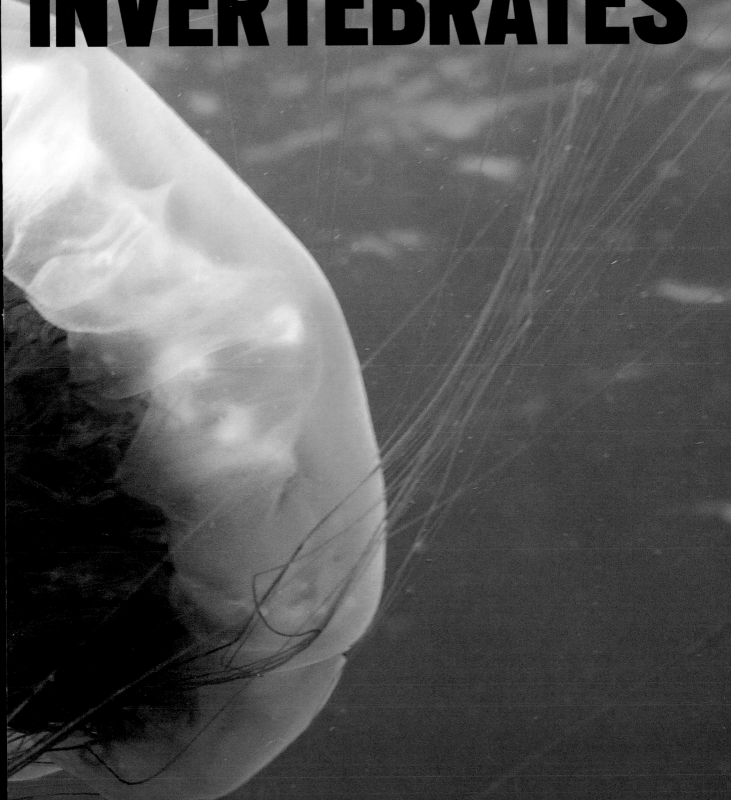

WORLD'S LARGEST JELLYFISH

The title of world's largest jellyfish is claimed by the Lion's Mane Jellyfish, *Cyanea capillata*, which occurs in the North Atlantic, North Pacific and Arctic Oceans. The largest specimen ever recorded had a body that was 2.7m (9ft) in diameter, which means that even a grown human could have lain on top of it. That, however, would be a bad idea, because the predatory Lion's Mane has stinging tentacles, and if you were exposed to enough of a sting they could potentially kill you.

That same outsize specimen, found in 1870, had tentacles that measured 37m (121ft) in length. If this is a reliable measurement, then the Lion's Mane has a claim to be the world's longest animal of any kind (although some marine worms may exceed that).

LONGEST PENIS

The much-coveted prize for the longest penis in the animal kingdom belongs to the group of stationary crustaceans known as barnacles (subclass Cirripedia), which are very common on seashores throughout the world. Barnacles have been described as "nothing more than a little shrimp-like animal standing on its head in a limestone house and kicking food into its mouth." They are absolutely immovable, stuck fast to rocks, so reproduction can be difficult. To succeed, they have to mate with a near-neighbour that is functionally of the opposite sex (don't ask), meaning that they have to do some investigation work, so to speak, with the penis. The penis is considerably longer than the whole body, and liable to stretch to about 10 times the body length. Once it has done its work, the penis withers, falls off and a new one is formed next year.

PREVIOUS PAGES: The Lion's Mane Jellyfish is the largest of its kind.
LEFT: Box jellyfishes can be deadly, a problem exacerbated by their almost transparent appearance.
RIGHT: The barnacle is the unlikely winner of the coveted world's longest penis award.

WORLD'S MOST DEADLY JELLYFISH

It is well worth giving any jellyfish a wide berth, because many have venom and sometimes this can cause severe pain. In terms of victims, though, there is no doubt that the box jellyfish, of which there are several species, are the most dangerous, causing a number of human fatalities every year. The venom of the commonest Australian species, *Chironex fleckeri*, can apparently kill you within four minutes if you are exposed to enough poison. It could be the most poisonous animal in the world.

Box jellyfish differ from other jellyfish in that the body (or medusa) is roughly cube-shaped. They are also, unfortunately, almost transparent, which makes them particularly dangerous.

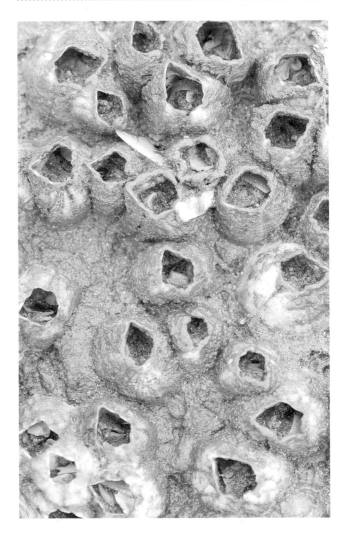

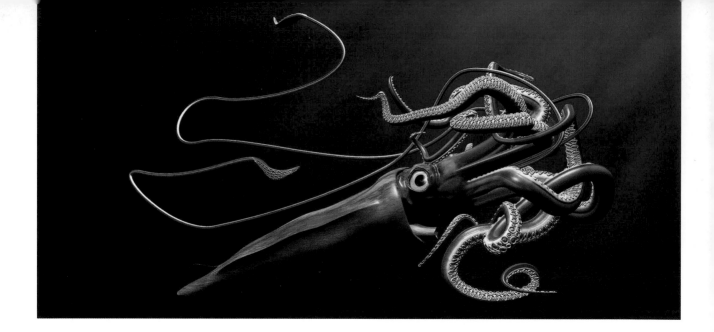

LARGEST EYE

The largest eyes in the animal kingdom belong to a mollusc, the Colossal Squid, *Mesonychoteuthis hamiltoni*, a poorly known animal that lives at great depths in the southern oceans. A well-preserved specimen examined in 2008 was found to have eyes 27cm (11in) in diameter, so the size of a football. Not far behind are the eyes of the Giant Squid, *Architeuthis dux* (above), which have been measured at 25cm (10in) but might sometimes be as big as the Colossal Squid's. Apart from the eyes, the question is: What are they going to call the next big squid species they find? The Huge Squid?

Bearing in mind that the next largest eyes in the animal kingdom are those of a swordfish, and that these are only 9cm (3.5in) in diameter, why is it that squids have such enormous eyes? The answer lies in detecting the approach of their major predator, the Great Sperm Whale, *Physeter macrocephalus*, in the ocean depths. Big eyes aren't particularly good at detecting faint light filtering down from the ocean surface, but what they are truly excellent at is detecting large luminous objects. Sperm whales aren't luminous themselves, but when they brush past high densities of tiny planktonic animals, they trigger bioluminescence all around them, including in their wake. It is this light that the squids are able to detect.

Incidentally, although the eyes of large squids are probably the largest that have ever existed, those of certain species of the extinct marine reptiles known as ichthyosaurs could possibly have been still larger.

MOST DEADLY HARPOONS

Beware the deadly cone snails (subfamily Coninae). These marine molluscs are renowned for their fabulously coloured and patterned shells (right), with sumptuous designs that wouldn't look out of place in a catalogue of fine pottery or clothes. In life, however, they are highly venomous predators, and they can and do kill people when accidentally touched. The largest species are up to 23cm (9.1in) long.

Cone snails eat a variety of prey, including worms, other molluscs and fish. Being snails they aren't fast-moving, but they don't need to be, because they can instantaneously paralyse their prey using, of all things, a harpoon. And even more bizarrely, that harpoon is a modified tooth on the animal's 'tongue,' or radula. They use one tooth at a time for each harpoon.

These snails detect their food with their siphon, which is like a nose. When something registers, they extend their proboscis forward towards the prey, and as soon as they touch it they shoot the venom-covered harpoon into the flesh. Alternatively, they may extend their mouth forward and encircle smaller fish, in the fashion of a net, and then harpoon what they need. Either way, the prey is swallowed whole. It is highly likely that the snails release a chemical into the water to slow the fish down first; these predators also hunt at night, when fish are asleep.

One of the more surprising things about cone snails is the sheer toxicity of their venom. It is generally a concoction of hundreds of different chemicals, and every one of the 600 species has a different set of toxins. A few of these have been incorporated into medicine, used as compounds for pain relief.

MOST ABUNDANT ANIMAL

It will always be nigh-on impossible to know what the most abundant animal on earth is, especially since there can be thousands of invertebrates in a teaspoon full of soil.

However, in terms of what can be measured, a good candidate is a crustacean known as *Euphausia superba*, the Antarctic Krill. It lives in the rich oceans around the Antarctic and feeds on plant plankton (phytoplankton). Swarms of krill can contain as many as 30,000 animals per cubic metre (35 cubic feet), enough to sustain the great whales such as the Blue Whale, which take krill as their main diet.

A recent estimate put the total biomass of Antarctic Krill as 500 million tons. If each animal weighs 2g (0.07oz), that equates to 500,000 animals per ton. So altogether that is... a lot of individuals.

HARDEST PUNCH BY AN ANIMAL

There are two types of mantis shrimps (order Stomatopoda). That these are colloquially known as 'spearers' and 'smashers' gives you some idea of what mantis shrimps are like. You would not want to start an argument with one in a pub. These lobster-like crustaceans are well-armed, belligerent and have exceptionally keen eyesight.

Another thing you mustn't do with certain types of mantis shrimp is to keep them in a glass aquarium. That's because they can smash through glass, which could make a mess. Oh, and you wouldn't want to pick them up unless you were exceedingly careful, either. Their name derives from their two front claws, which are held coiled at the chest in a faint resemblance to a praying mantis. And these claws uncoil and punch forward at a simply mid-boggling rate of acceleration, equivalent to 10,400 g-force, or 102,000 metres per second squared (m/s^2). Bearing in mind that the claws may also have a cutting edge, it is no wonder that a few strikes from a mantis shrimp can leave a prey item literally shredded. In fact, each blow hits the victim twice, once directly and once with a shock wave caused by the creation of instantaneous bubbles between the waters and the claws, which then collapse violently. These predators can eat almost any prey animal of appropriate size, including molluscs, whose shells they can smash. Australians, with their typical straight-talking, call them 'prawn-killers'.

Mantis shrimps occur throughout the oceans but are commonest in the tropics, and they are generally quite retiring and hard to see, living among rocks. In some parts of the world they are eaten, and apparently pack quite a punch.

....

OPPOSITE AND NEXT PAGE: Mantis shrimps are extraordinary crustaceans blessed with some bizarre gifts. Many are exquisitely colourful, and their own colour vision is quite probably the best of any animal anywhere in the world. In addition, they can punch so hard with their forelimbs that they can break the glass of an aquarium, and literally shred their prey.

MOST STYLISH ESCAPE MECHANISM

You might not have heard of ostracods (class Ostracoda), since they are very small crustaceans that inhabit the metaphorical backstreets of both the freshwater and marine environments. There are hundreds of species, some of which live in the deeper parts of the sea, where no sunlight ever penetrates. The only relief comes from chemical reactions inside the bodies of the animals, known as bioluminescence.

Why should animals light themselves up in this way? In most cases it is for defence purposes. When an ostracod is swallowed by a fish, for example, it gives off a very strong pulse of blue light caused by the compounds luciferin and luciferase mixing together and producing something akin to a small firework. Almost invariably the predator spits out the ostracod.

It probably isn't the shock of swallowing the flashy crustacean that causes the fish to react in this way, but self-preservation instead. A fish lit-up so strongly is itself a magnet for predators, a deer in the headlights. So it expels the danger.

....

BEST EYESIGHT

On the subject of mantis shrimps (see previous page), their super-fast forelimbs are not their only extraordinary attribute. Their eyes, which are on stalks, have the most remarkable vision. This covers the same colours that we see, plus ultraviolet and polarised light. It would be difficult for us even to appreciate just what a kaleidoscope of hues these animals see, since we only have three types of colour-receptive cones, while mantis shrimps have no less than 16.

LONGEST TIME LOOKING AFTER EGGS

Probably the last creature that you'd expect to set this record is the one that actually has set it – an octopus. Perhaps this is because most people don't realise that octopuses look after their eggs at all. However, that is exactly what they do, and a deep-sea octopus known as *Graneleone boreopacifica* has recently been recorded looking after her eggs for four and a half *years*. She carried out this feat 1,400m (4,600ft) below the surface in Monterey Canyon, off the coast of California, USA.

Perhaps this animal's most remarkable feat isn't the fact that she attended the eggs for so long, protecting them from predators and making sure that they were kept clean, but that she might not have fed very much, or even at all, during all of that time. When observed, the octopus did not attempt to snatch any of the abundant food in the vicinity, and over the years was observed to lose weight and for her skin to become loose and pale.

There was a happy ending, though. The eggs hatched – all 160 of them.

BEST REGENERATION

Sea cucumbers (class Holothuroidea) are a group of marine organisms related to starfish. They look like large sausages (above), or perhaps legless caterpillars, and live on the sea-bed, sometimes at great depths. Some of the things that they do with their bodies are scarcely believable.

You might have heard that starfish are masters of regeneration; if a five-armed starfish accidently loses a couple of limbs to a predator, it will simply grow its arms back in time. More bizarrely, some starfish reproduce asexually by simply breaking apart, with one half putting up two arms to the other's three! Following the traditions of their echinoderm relatives, sea cucumbers will also split by fission, but in their case they literally tear themselves apart, with each half going its own separate way.

However, it is in defence that sea cucumbers really show the world how to regenerate. When attacked they can almost explode in a mass of body parts. Some discharge from their anus a mass of sticky threads that entangle predators, threads that once formed part of their own respiration system. Others more or less eviscerate, expelling bits of gut, gonad and respiratory organ in a cloud, leaving the 'shell' of the body to escape while the predator eats the rest. And some other species just seem to disintegrate. Yet in all these cases, all the necessary bits and pieces regrow, often within a few weeks.

MOST EYES

When you think about the animal on earth with the most eyes, your mind simply isn't going to suddenly come up with 'scallops, of course!' But in terms of the number of functioning eyes as we know them, these marine bivalves (family Pectinidae) come up trumps. Some have more than 100 eyes, and they are blue. Each eye has a retina, they all have a lens and they are all connected to the optic nerve. They even possess a tapetum, a disc that reflects light back (like the eyes of a cat) and on to the photoreceptors.

The eyes are fixed on to the animal's mantle (see above) and, if you imagine a scallop with its two shells almost shut, they are placed in the slit between the two. They are highly efficient in detecting both light and movement in the water where the scallop lives.

The scallop's relative, the Giant Clam, *Tridachna gigas*, also has 'eyes' on its mantle, sometimes thousands. But these are much simpler and are really little more than photo-receptors without lenses, so for the moment the scallop's eyes have it.

UTHER INVERTEBRATES

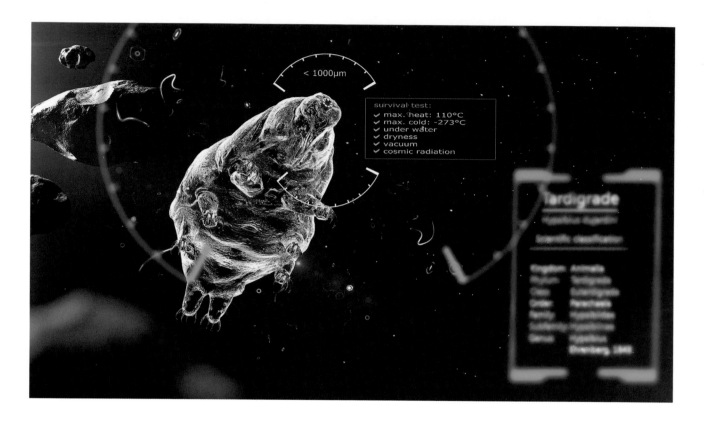

< 1000μm

survival test:
✔ max. heat: 110°C
✔ max. cold: -273°C
✔ under water
✔ dryness
✔ vacuum
✔ cosmic radiation

Tardigrade

MOST TOLERANT ORGANISMS

In a book about extreme animals, you could hardly miss out a group of organisms that are colloquially known as extremophiles, those that positively thrive in ludicrously adverse conditions. It turns out that the most extreme of extremophiles are an obscure group known as tardigrades, or 'water bears' (above). These small – usually about 0.5mm (0.02in) long – segmented animals, in a special division (phylum) all of their own, have eight legs and live in water. What makes them remarkable is the ability to withstand almost any kind of abuse. Think of the cartoon character that survives being blown up, drowning, falling from a great height, having a car fall on it – such is the survivability of a tardigrade.

For a start they can go without food or water for up to 10 years. They are so temperature tolerant that they can be frozen down to one degree of absolute zero, so -273°C (-459°F), and then unfreeze again undaunted. They can be heated to beyond the boiling point of water and still survive. They can be subject to 6000x atmospheric pressure and 1000x what would be a lethal dose of radiation for any other animal. They survive various poisons and toxins. You wouldn't want an infestation in your house.

Next we will hear that they can survive outer space. Well actually, they can. Tardigrades have been taken up in a spaceship and survived in the vacuum of space for no less than 10 days. Yet these are real, living animals, present in a small clump of moss near you.

Not a happy ending for the rodent, but the *Toxoplasma* is going home.

MOST SINISTER MANIPULATION OF A HOST

Toxoplasma gondii is a protozoan parasite that is almost ubiquitous, affecting a wide range of warm-blooded animals, including humans. However, although it can reproduce asexually in every host, in order to reproduce sexually, and thereby complete its lifecycle, it needs to enter the guts of a cat.

T. gondii routinely affects Brown Rats, *Rattus norvegicus*, as opposed to cats, and when this happens, it seems that the protozoan has evolved to sense an opportunity. While rats normally avoid cats, and are adept at recognising their signs, it seems that rats with a *Toxoplasma* infection no longer do this. In fact, it is quite the opposite; despite themselves, the rats' perception of cat risk is somehow manipulated and they become attracted to cats instead. Not surprisingly, this defect means that the rats frequently end up in the cat's intestines – and that, for the protozoan, is the perfect destination.

SHORTEST LIFESPAN

Aside from bacteria, which may live for just a few minutes, the creatures with the shortest complete lifespan are known as gastrotrichs. These are microscopic, worm-like creatures which live in the muck at the bottom of ponds or the sea. If you've never heard of them, fear not, your life hasn't been wasted; gastrotrichs don't set the world alight. They don't do much except eat detritus and bacteria, and reproduce. They mature at astonishing speed, and some are 'born' and die within a span of three days.

FURTHER READING

Couzens, D., *Extreme Birds*, HarperCollins Publishers, 2008.

Del Hoyo, J., Elliott, A., Sargatal, J. & Christie, D.A. (eds.), *Handbook of the Birds of the World, Volumes 1-16*, Lynx Edicions, Barcelona, 1992-2011.

Fuller, E., *The Passenger Pigeon*, Princeton University Press, 2015.

Halliday, T. & Adler, K., *The New Encyclopedia of Reptiles and Amphibians*, Oxford University Press, 2002.

Loon, R. & L., *Birds: The Inside Story*, Struik, 2005.

MacDonald, D.W., *The Encyclopedia of Mammals*, Oxford University Press, 2006.

Matisson, C., *Frogs and Toads*, Natural History Museum, London, 2011.

Newton, I., *The Migration Ecology of Birds*, Academic Press, 2008.

Naylor, P., *Great British Marine Animals* (Third Edition), Sound Diving Productions, 2011.

Perrins, C. (ed.), *The New Encyclopedia of Birds*, Oxford University Press, 2003.

Resh, V.H. & Cardé, R.T. (eds.), *Encyclopedia of Insects*, Academic Press, 2003.

Wilson, D.E. & Mittermeier, R.A. (eds.), *Handbook of the Mammals of the Worlds, Volumes 1-4*, Lynx Edicions, Barcelona, 2009-15.

WEBSITES

http://entnemdept.ufl.edu/walker/ufbir/chapters/index_order.shtml

http://www.wikipedia.org/

ABOUT THE AUTHOR

Website: www.birdwords.co.uk

Twitter: @DominicCouzens

DEDICATION

This book is dedicated to my wife Carolyn and children Emmie and Sam.

ACKNOWLEDGEMENTS

With thanks to Simon Papps, my publisher at Reed New Holland, and Thomas Casey, who designed this book.

IMAGE CREDITS

(l = left, r = right, a = above, b = below, c = centre, i = inset)
All images by Dreamstime.com (individual photographer credits in brackets):

Front cover a (Cathy Keifer); Front cover b (Mgkuijpers); Back cover a (Ralph Lohse); Back cover bl (Faunuslsd); Back cover bc (Bob Suir); Back cover br (Vjrithwik); 1 (Mikael Males); 2-3 (Isselee); 4-5 (Steven Oehlenschlager); 6-7, 136-137 (Dmirijs Mihejevs); 7b, 12-13r (filedimage); 8-9, 80ai (Jezbennett); 10-11 (Volodymyr Byrdyak); 13 (Sdbower); 14-15 (Michael Lynch); 16-17 (Fiifre); 17 inset (Lorraine Swanson); 18a (Cuna); 18b (Mr1805); 20 (Marco Lijoi); 21 (Vladyslav Morozov); 22 (Richard Gerrish); 23al (Pablo Caridad); 23ar, 50-51, 63r, 69a (Mike Lane); 23b (Amilevin); 24-25 (András Sipos); 25i (Naturablichter); 26ia (Kjetil Kolbjornsrud); 26ib (Oleg Znamenskiy); 26-27 (Ongchangwei); 28 (Sburel); 29 (Aughty Venable); 30 (Mr 1805); 31 (Geoffrey Kuchera); 32-33, 33ia (Sergey Uryadnikov); 34 (Tony Campbell); 35 (Outdoorsman); 36 (S100apm); 37 (Sprague Theobald); 38-39 (Bob Suir); 40-41 (Anthony Aneese Totah Jr); 41il (Reinout Van Wagtendonk); 41ir (Ericg1970); 42al (Paul Banton); 42ar (Andreanita); 42b (Kierran Allen); 44i (Dmytro Pylypenko); 44-45 (Mcasabar); 46-47 (Erectus); 48-49 (Wkruck); 52a, 52b (Maximilian Buzun); 54l, 78, 79l (Duncan Noakes); 54-55 (Fullempty); 56il (John Carnemolla); 56ir (Paul Reeves); 56-57 (Boris Belchev); 58-59 (Foxyjoshi); 59a (Claire Fulton); 60 (Karelgallas); 61a, 61b (Danie Malan); 62 (Vladimir Seliverstov); 63l (Pablo Mendez Rodriguez); 64 (Joan Egert); 65 (Hakoar); 66 (Bluesunphoto); 67 (Alptraum); 68-69 (Mlarduengo); 71 (Stu Porter); 72-73 (Faizan Khan); 74l, 82-83, 102-103 (Feathercollector); 74r (Urospoteko); 75a, 144-145 (Nico Smit); 75b (Rusty Dodson); 76 (Meisterphotos); 77l (Luc Sesselle); 77r (Belizar); 79r (Teckken Tan); 80-81 (Mogens Trolle); 84-85 (Susan Robinson); 86-87, 96-97 (Cathy Keifer); 88i, 88-89 (Vjrithwik); 90 (Awcnz62); 91a (Timothy Lubcke); 91b (Speciestime); 92 (Jordi Prat Puig); 93l (Mracka); 93r, 95b (Corey A Ford); 94 (Ralph Lohse); 95a (Seanyu); 98 (Kjersti Joergensen); 99 (Cobia); 100 (Pablo Hidalgo); 101 (Designpicssub); 104a (Palych); 104-105 (Chris Hill); 106-107, 108 (Mgkuijpers); 107r (Daniel Halfmann); 109 (Antares614); 110 (Dmitry Maslov); 111 (Lukas Blazek); 112-113, 114 (Krzysztof Odziomek); 116l (Seatraveler); 116-117 (Martin Eager); 118-119 (Jamen Percy); 120 (Kampee Patisena); 121l (Andamanse); 121r (Alexander Ogurtsov); 122-123 (Carol Buchanan); 124-125 (Steve Byland); 126-127 (Mr Smith Chetanachan); 128-129 (Joseph Calev); 130-131 (Holger Leyrer); 131r (Mario Madrona Barrera); 132l (Alexandr Mitiuc); 132-133 (Vladvitek); 134 (Horia Vlad Bogdan); 138l (Albertoloyo); 138r (Julia Freeman-woolpert); 139a (Photographerlondon); 139b (Paul Sparks); 140l (John Braid); 140-141 (Faunuslsd); 142 (Dtguy); 143 (Surut Wattanamaetee); 146-147 (Edward Phillips); 147a (Lawcain); 148-149 (Hakoar); 150-151 (Stevenrussellsmithphotos); 153 (Howard Nevitt Jr); 154-155 (Gergely Zsolnai); 156-157 (Danolsen); 158 (Mjkuijpers); 159 (Andamanse); 160-161 (Crispi); 162-163 (Stig Karlsson); 164-165 (Steven Melanson); 166 (R. Gino Santa Maria/Shutterfree, Llc); 167 (Zygotehasnobrain); 168 (Paul Fleet); 169 (Tim Heusinger Von Waldegge); 170-171 (Dmytro Pylypenko); 173 (Kjersti Joergensen); 174-175 (Beverly Speed); 176 (Ericsch); 177 (Asther Lau Choon Siew); 178 (Stefanie Winkler); 179 (Vallorie Francis).

INDEX

bold = image